Still an Inconvenient Youth

Julius Malema carries on

Fiona Forde

PICADOR AFRICA

First published in 2011 by Picador Africa
an imprint of Pan Macmillan South Africa
Private Bag X19, Northlands, Johannesburg, 2116

This edition published in 2014 by Picador Africa

www.panmacmillan.co.za

ISBN 978-1-77010-396-2
eBook ISBN 978-1-77010-397-9

Proofreading by Lisa Compton
Design and typesetting by Manoj Sookai
Cover photograph by Mujahid Safodien (© AFP ImageForum)
Cover by MR Design

Printed and bound by Creda Communications

Contents

Foreword to
An Inconvenient Youth

This Foreword was originally written for the 2011 edition of this book, An Inconvenient Youth, *at a time when Julius Malema was at the peak of his career in the ANC. Despite the turn that events have taken and the shift in focus towards the EFF in this new edition, Achille Mbembe's concepts remain relevant as we attempt to understand the Malema phenomenon in 2014. It is with Mbembe's permission that we republish it here.*

This unusually bold and astutely written book retraces the multiple paths of Julius Malema's rise as one of the most controversial political figures of post-apartheid South Africa. Rich in its insights and original in its perspectives, it is a major contribution to our understanding of the multilayered lives and intricate workings of the African National Congress (ANC) as the former national liberation movement, now the ruling party, struggles with power, with itself and with the idea of South Africa.

Fiona Forde shows how the oldest modern political organisation in Africa has mutated into a patchwork of unstable, segmented and shifting networks of interests less and less united

by principle or ideology and more and more bound by ruthless expediency.

Born and raised in poverty, Julius Malema is at once atypical and symptomatic of his times. He embodies both the passions and contradictions of post-struggle politics and the dark and troubling undercurrents of a long South African tradition of lumpen radicalism.

Lumpen radicalism is a political tradition of unruliness – and at times resistance – in which fantasies of male power, control and desire have always been deeply entangled with 'war envy' and an almost insatiable appetite for money, luxuries and women.

It is a direct product of the influx-control system, the mass forced removals and relocations, and the relentless and all-pervading social and economic insecurity that became the hallmarks of black urban experience under apartheid.

A hybrid cultural and political style the ANC did not hesitate to instrumentalise during the struggle, but which it safely kept at the margins of the liberation movement's core ethos, it is also a tradition in which acts of pseudo-revolutionary rage are mixed with various forms of care.

Within this tradition, power is first conquered on the street before it is translated into the domain of home and formal institutions. A life of shame, social humiliation and dishonour is thought to be retrieved from abjection through conspicuous display and consumption of wealth.

Politics is less about the patient and disciplined building of a civic ethos than about the performance of mob power while cohorts, cliques, gangs or, eventually, the crowd stand for 'the people' or 'the masses'.

A distinctive feature of lumpen radicalism in South African politics since the formation of the ANC in 1912 has been the

cyclical re-emergence of the youth as a force across the social and cultural landscape.

The ascendancy of the youth, its attempt to wrestle power from the older generation and to take charge of the adults, has usually coincided with periods of intense fracture of the black life experience and the concomitant crisis of imagination within the liberation movement.

During the twentieth century, three such notable episodes stand out. The first happened in the early 1950s when, under pressure from the Youth League, the ANC adopted increasingly radical positions that ultimately led to the turn to the armed struggle.

The second was the Soweto uprising in 1976. The third was the phenomenon of the 'comrades' in the 1980s when the apartheid state's hold over the township was weakened. Vast urban zones were declared 'ungovernable'. In many townships, state power was replaced by popular civic structures and, in a dramatic reversal of apartheid urban planning, informal settlements and shacks sprawled out in all directions.

Today, a similar crisis of imagination is at work in the party, in society and in culture. One of the main tensions within South African politics today is the realisation that there is something unresolved in the constitutional democratic settlement that suspended the 'revolution' in 1994 but did not erase apartheid once and for all from the social, economic and mental landscape.

For each of the historical protagonists in the South African drama, this settlement resulted in no final victory and no crippling defeat. Seventeen years later, the country is still caught between an intractable present and an irrecoverable past; things that are no longer and things that are not yet.

This is ironically the stalemate many hailed as 'the South African miracle'. It is the stalemate Malema would like to

puncture. It is in the failure of South African government and society to build creatively on the extraordinary rupture, or promise, of 1994 and radically confront black poverty that Malema sees his political opportunity.

His ascendancy highlights the current dangers South Africa faces: a gradual closing of life chances for many; an increasing polarisation of the racial structure; a structure of indecision at the heart of politics itself; and a re-balkanisation of culture and society. These trends clearly undermine the fragile forms of mutuality that have been painstakingly built in South Africa over a decade and a half and further weaken the prospects of true non-racialism.

The signs of entropy are there for all to see. They are particularly dramatised by the dilemmas of unemployment and the expansion of spaces of vulnerability in all arenas of everyday life. Despite the emergence of a solid black middle class, a rising superfluous population is becoming a permanent fixture of the South African social fabric with little possibility of ever being exploited by capital.

Most young black youth are barely holding on to the ledge. They are likely never to get full-time formal employment or to enter the proletarian economy. Stuck in a field of blighted possibilities, they scavenge to live or simply to get through the day – so many bad jobs available to so few in one of the most racially unequal countries on earth; so much rage and almost no future.

For those in survival mode – and who know all too well what it means to experience social humiliation first-hand – Julius Malema fills the gaps of disappointment and failure at a time when the promise of liberation has become privatised and the

ideals of reciprocity and mutuality enshrined in the Constitution are struggling to find the political and cultural platforms they deserve.

His stock is rising in a landscape of ruins: the ideological bankruptcy of the official Left; the racial and class narcissism of the main opposition party; and an ANC consumed by corruption and greed, brutal internecine battles for power and a deadly combination of predatory instincts and intellectual vacuity.

To stem the rising tide, technocratic sermons on 'service delivery' and 'decent jobs' will not suffice.

Techno-managerial reason will have to be supplemented by the rehabilitation of the political itself, that is, the conscious engagement with the fundamental choices that will determine the nature of the South African experiment in democracy: questions of how to right historical wrongs; the relationship between personal or collective injury and larger problems of equality and dignity; private ownership and the right to a fair share of the nation's wealth; freedom from race and racism.

It is the widespread failure to confront these fundamental dilemmas that has created the moral void in which Julius Malema is swimming. The shock troops he is assembling before the final push are replete with those imprisoned in shack life, vulnerable subjects our unequal social order keeps ejecting, who are condemned to undertake the labour of social mourning amid crushing poverty.

To all of them, he promises an unworkable mirage: nationalisation of mines, land expropriation without compensation, economic emancipation and control over resources they do not own.

For the democratic project to have any future at all in South Africa, politics should break with the depressive realism that has characterised post-apartheid life.

It should not simply attend to the feeling many have of having been defeated. It should be about reopening the future for all. More radically, it should take the form of a conscious attempt to retrieve life and the human from a long history of waste.

Achille Mbembe
Cape Town, July 2011

Preface

No sooner does one write the name 'Julius Malema' than a host of bold and bellicose images spring to mind, but when I first met him towards the end of 2007 he was not half the moxie character he is today and, at the age of twenty-six, he was still relatively unknown. It was around the middle of November, just a few weeks ahead of the African National Congress's (ANC's) landmark elections that would bring Jacob Zuma to power, a presidency that would in time also propel Malema to the party's front line. It didn't take long until he began trading as a populist, typically full of empty promises, and within no time at all he was the talking point of the country.

Yet there was no real understanding of who he was or what he really stood for and so, in 2009, as a reporter for one of the country's newspapers, I 'shadowed' Malema for a week to try to capture a clearer picture of who was lurking behind the headlines. I remember sitting in his office, which by then was in the ANC headquarters in downtown Johannesburg, trying to reach an agreement with him about what it was I wanted to achieve when he turned to me, momentarily confused, and asked: 'About this shadowing thing, does it mean that you'll be there but I won't know it?'

To his credit, he agreed and that brief 'window' opened my eyes wide to the phenomenon that is Malema. It led me to write the first edition of this book, *An Inconvenient Youth*, an unauthorised biography for which he generously granted me access to him over a period of two years.

But as luck would have it, Malema's life began to fill with more drama than a comic book in that time: his lifestyle began to raise the suspicions of the revenue collector the year that I began my research; his businesses fell under the spotlight of the serious crimes office a year later; the office of the Public Protector was called in to check him out; five days after the first edition hit the shelves, he received his first serious warning from the ANC for his outlandish political behaviour; and by the time the international edition was launched in London in 2012, the luckless youth leader had been turfed out of the party.

And lo. Two years on Malema was swaggering through the doors of parliament as the head of the Economic Freedom Fighters (EFF), the socialist party he founded when he was no longer welcome in Zuma's ANC. He is still every bit the populist but more deft a politician than ever before. And yet there is still an element of telltale confusion, if not ignorance, among many South Africans about how he could make such a spectacular comeback on the back of the country's underclass. Either they underestimate him or the seething anger that is out there or they are living in total and utter denial.

But going back to 2009, it was also then that the Nigerian writer Chimamanda Ngozi Adichie addressed a gathering in Oxford. She talked about the 'single story' and the dangers of interpreting life or people through a narrow lens. To make her point, she went back to her childhood.

She grew up in Nsukka, the town that is home to the University of Nigeria, where her father was a professor and her mother a university registrar. As a young girl she was an avid reader, but her middle-class upbringing exposed her to American rather than African children's books. When she started dabbling with her own short stories she found she was mentally locked into the characters and tales she had read about. She wouldn't understand why until many years later.

Her opening words would always be followed by characters 'who were white and blue-eyed. They played in the snow. They ate apples. And they talked a lot about the weather, how lovely it was that the sun came up,' she remembered. All this despite the fact that she had never set foot outside Nigeria.

'We didn't have snow. We ate mangoes. And we never talked about the weather because there was no need.

'I did not know that people like me could exist in literature,' she continued. 'I had become convinced that books, by their very nature, had to have foreigners in them. And had to be about things with which I could not personally identify.'

All that changed when she began to read Chinua Achebe, her fellow countryman, as well as other African writers. That was when she realised that 'people like me, girls with skin the colour of chocolate, with kinky hair that could not form ponytails, could also exist in literature'. That was when her 'single story' began to take on a new dimension.

But the 'single story' went beyond books and coloured Chimamanda's upbringing in other ways. She gave the example of Fide, her family's 'houseboy' as she referred to him.

He came from a very poor background and when, as a child, Chimamanda would not finish the food on her plate, her mother would remind her that 'people like Fide don't have food at all'.

Chimamanda heard it so often that she began to attach a single identity to Fide: poverty.

A few years later she accompanied Fide to the villages to visit his family. To her shock, she found his brother weaving a beautiful basket. She could not connect what Fide's brother was doing with the mental image she had crafted of Fide's world, because the lens through which she viewed him was so narrow and singular that she couldn't imagine his family as anything other than poor. Creativity didn't fit into the box into which she had placed Fide.

'Poverty was my single story of them.'

Years later she found herself at the other end of the narrow lens when she went to the United States. Her university roommate was surprised to find that Chimamanda could speak English fluently, ignorant of the fact that it is the official language in Nigeria. She was also disappointed when Chimamanda whipped out her Mariah Carey CD after she had asked to listen to her 'tribal music'.

'She had a single story of Africa.'

Julius Malema's early political career was also viewed through a very narrow lens, his life and times recorded by way of a 'single story'.

His followers cast him as a victim, a freedom fighter whose bravery was becoming his biggest bane, a man whose ideas were unsettling the status quo. They didn't see his wealth as conspicuous. They saw him instead as a young African who had 'landed', much to the fury of the whites. It was a harmless hero that was captured through their lens.

A different single story was crafted by his detractors, who placed him into a box that varied from politically dangerous to

radical, racist, bigoted, stupid, corrupt, ignorant, and so on, each of the attributes woven into a damning, dark tale.

Like Fide, a single identity was always attached to Malema.

Though partly accurate, it was neither comprehensive nor complete.

Perhaps it was as Adichie had said: some people couldn't personally identify with him so they misplaced him instead.

Yet in the time I spent with him in the course of researching the first edition of this book, I found my way inside his head and encountered a character whom I liked, irrespective of the politician. Malema could be sensitive, witty, humorous, thoughtful even, in the strictest sense of the word. He was a calculating person. He was also open-minded enough to engage in conversations of all sorts and he was generally good company.

But there was a side to him that was extraordinarily wily and cunning and it was there that the overlap between the man and the politician began to emerge.

As a politician, Malema disturbed me and continues to do so. In his public appearances I couldn't see the person I had come to know in private. It didn't surprise me that he was razor sharp as a political strategist – I had always found him to be extremely clever. But it was the sulphurous relationship he developed with much of society that unsettled me. White South Africans were always placed in the firing line of his political messages, his weapons of mass destruction. The Convention for a Democratic South Africa (CODESA) talks of the early 1990s were intended to lay such retaliation to rest, but then all these years later along came this raffish youth from a township called Seshego, a place many of them had never heard of, a place in South Africa that is so far from their cosy worlds that it could well be situated in some far-off country.

Perhaps it was arrogance that had allowed a large portion of white South Africa to assume they would never have to give the Seshegos of this country a second careful thought. Township and suburban life are poles apart in this African country and the comfortable suburban dweller would not last half a day on the other side of township life. Townships are uncomfortable, densely populated places. They reek of poverty and general desperation and ghastly social ills. Unemployment is rife and the young and the old who saunter their streets for hours on end each day are living reminders of that. Of course some do draw a living wage and some more make it to a modest existence, but the vast majority of the townships' people live the kind of lives that urban folk cannot even begin to contemplate.

It is on the back of that raw socio-economic divide that Malema is now spearheading his populist juggernaut through the heart of South Africa, but it is madness on his part to ascribe that singular and narrow reasoning to the country's challenges. South Africa's story is not a single story: the whites are not the problem; they are merely, or in most instances at least, the epitome of it. The problem is far greater than five or six million pale-skinned folk. The country is fundamentally unworkable and it is almost irrelevant whether it is whites or blacks or a mix of the two that sit at either side of that taut divide because structurally the country is in a mess.

The ANC tends to dismiss the current challenges with a promise of 'the second phase of the transition', as if it alone will root out and solve the weighty socio-economic problems. For sure, this is not only a glib and meaningless message but one that is loaded with an assumption that those who have been sat on for too long are willing to hang around another while.

Instead it is Malema, the *beau idéal* of the underclass, who is turning this tide in a moment of overbred despair, and there can

be no small doubt about the sordid way things are tending with a figure so feckless at the helm. And I say that with a fair degree of knowing.

My aspiration in writing this latest unauthorised edition of his story is to explain the Malema phenomenon. I see him as one of the most extraordinary political figures of modern South Africa. I know him to be a man of many faces, someone who ticks a great number of the boxes on the register of humanity, as Achille Mbembe puts it elswhere. But Malema is as complex as South Africa's story itself is and, like it, he is a hugely controversial product of one hundred years of struggle politics.

Fiona Forde
Johannesburg, July 2014

Between the idea
And the reality
Between the motion
And the act
Falls the Shadow

(T.S. Eliot, 'The Hollow Men', 1925)

Chapter 1

Populism in drag

Never one to play a shy hand, Julius Malema, or Mao-lema as his party hacks call him, took the South African parliament by storm on the day he was sworn in. It was 21 May, a fortnight after the 2014 general elections in which his new socialist party won twenty-five seats on the back of more than a million votes. To hammer home their victory, the Economic Freedom Fighters (EFF) decided to take their revolution to parliament. The men waded into the national assembly wearing bright red workers' overalls, hard hats and gumboots while the women wore the traditional gear of the 'home help'. A first for the South African parliament, without a doubt, but this was playtime for the populists.

It wasn't the first time that Malema had stuffed his ample frame into the ill-fitting onesie with his paunch forcing the stiff cloth to gather around his fat buttocks. The overalls made their debut at some stage along the election campaign when he began to talk up his revolution, promising a lifelong socialist festival to the poor if they would dare trust him with their hard-earned vote.

But there was something so utterly false about it all. What kind of a hardened revolutionary would feel the need to dress up for the part, to borrow the working-man's clothes in a mechanical

attempt to make his message work? Though the overalls were the perfect complement to the red berets, the signature caps of resistance that the EFFs adopted not long after their launch, the memories of Malema with his Breitling watches, designer shoes and flashy cars were still too fresh to fool anyone. He was like a populist in drag the day he became an MP.

The attire to one side, though, the rest is familiar territory for Malema. During his latter years in the African National Congress (ANC) when he pounded the tarmac extolling the virtues of the ruling party, he began selling the idea of a socialist South Africa. For him, it was the last stage of the National Democratic Revolution (NDR), the propagandistic screed by which the ANC stands but which few of its leaders dare mention in any kind of meaningful way in these modern times.

'We have three areas of strategic influence, which the NDR seeks to attain: political power, economic power and social power,' he once told me while at the peak of his power in the ANC, long before the EFF was even a flicker in his mind.

'We are at the beginning,' he answered, when I asked him to rate the progress of the so-called revolutionary project on a scale of one to ten.

'Nineteen-ninety-four was the ushering in of one of the aspects of the NDR, which is political power,' while social power towards 'a non-sexist, non-racial, democratic South Africa' is still a work in progress. The big one, economic power, was where his mind was focused then, when he began the call to nationalise the country's mineral resources.

'Is socialism the end stage of the NDR?' I asked.

'Yes,' he replied, even though the ANC would insist it was a multi-class, broad-church structure, rarely describing itself as a socialist party.

'We have a responsibility to safeguard the identity of the ANC as multi-class, an organisation that seeks to liberate our people,'

he said in defence. 'Our immediate task now is the liberation of our people in an economic sense. As to what happens after, we will decide.'

It was clear that some form of socialism was going to be the inevitable consequence of him wielding his way to power, even though then, around 2009 and 2010, socialism was a dirty word he only dared whisper.

'You see, people are afraid of the word "socialism" and you must not pronounce it a lot. It will scare them,' he was careful to explain. 'I might have houses. I might have watches. That's what the economic system dictates now. But when we've got an economic system that says that everything we have we need to bring together and share among ourselves, I will be the first one to surrender. I've got no problem with socialism. I've got a problem with socialists who want to hijack the ANC and without giving this phase of our revolution a chance to unfold. They want to take us immediately to socialism. That will have serious consequences.'

Yet look at him now, steering a socialist juggernaut at breakneck speed as the proud head of a party that describes itself as being of the Marxist-Leninist tradition and the Frantz Fanon school of thought.

If anyone was going to go there, it was always going to be Malema. For the past five or so years he has been shrewdly articulating the racial and social anger that continues to bubble beneath the surface of South African society. He dared say what many felt but could not bring themselves to put words to. He hit on society's raw nerve and simply thrived on the chaos he was creating because it was awakening a new kind of militancy among millions of South Africans, many of whom were falling into step behind him.

In many respects he assumed the role that Winnie Madikizela-Mandela had played many years before him while her then husband, Nelson, was serving life imprisonment. In much the same manner as Malema does now, Madikizela-Mandela fanned the flames in townships across South Africa, and as a wild revolutionary figure she preached to the masses with her rafter-raising words. Like him, she was fearless and radical and pushed too close to the edge.

Like her, he was a political entrepreneur and though he is now operating in an environment of ample opportunity, he is tapping into the same constituencies and appeals to the same mentality that she once did.

Just as the past is beginning to recede into history, Malema is bringing it back to life as he casts the minds of millions back to the struggle era, reminding them of what they fought for, who they fought against and why the battle is still far from over. Unwittingly or otherwise, he has started a social tug of war that is fiercely playing out in South Africa's interregnum.

That ancient term – 'interregnum' – was used to describe the period of time that lapsed between the death of a royal sovereign and the enthronement of a successor. It allowed for a break with the past and it harboured expectations of change that would eventually unfold during the *justitium,* or transition.

In the 1930s, the Italian philosopher Antonio Gramsci took the concept of the interregnum into socio-political thinking and used it to define extraordinary periods of social and political change during which 'new frames' that are being introduced to make the 'old frames' useless are still in the design stage. It is a period of limbo, a time when there is little clarity and hardly any knowing and when nothing is as yet complete.

'The old is dying, and the new cannot be born; in this interregnum there arises a great diversity of morbid symptoms,' Gramsci once argued.

In 1982, Nobel laureate the late Nadine Gordimer addressed the New York Institute for the Humanities and talked about 'living in the interregnum' in South Africa as apartheid was nearing an end.

'Historical coordinates don't fit life any longer; new ones, where they exist, have couplings not to the rulers, but to the ruled,' she contemplated.

All these years later and South Africans are yet again 'living in the interregnum', though it is different to the one Gordimer talked of. This period is often referred to by the ruling ANC as a second transition, but described by Malema as the coming revolution.

It is hard to credit that it is Malema, a populist ranter, who is attempting to define the new frame hollering through his hand-held megaphone. It is even more difficult to believe that there are a million and more people ready to afford him the chance. Most astounding of all, perhaps, is the fact that he is operating in an open terrain with not a single competitor in sight.

There is nothing to suggest that Malema will succeed, of course. But if one considers his life story, his fighting nerve and his fearless outlook, there is every good reason to believe he will die trying. This is no revolutionary simpleton.

Chapter 2

The devil wears Breitling

24 April 2010
Caracas, Venezuela

It's Saturday morning, shortly after 09h30, and for the past half-hour or so I've been watching the young delegates make their way down the stairs, out of the hotel and onto the single-decker bus parked out front at the foot of the sloping, lush lawns. But there's still no sign of Julius Malema, so I settle into my armchair and wait as the foyer slowly empties. The steady hum of the tens of thousands of cars that clog the streets of Caracas on Venezuela's dirt-cheap petrol can still be heard high up in the suburb of San Bernardino on the flanks of Mount Avila, but it's a dim noise that doesn't intrude. The air is hot and humid, but not unbearably so. And it is a comfortable lull that settles over Hotel Avila, a serene spot to while away some time.

The ease is broken only when the pert-breasted woman behind the reception desk begins to dole out the day's duties to her colleagues as her shift comes to an end, her stiletto-sharp voice carrying right across the foyer as she struts between the front office and the back. Minutes later she slings her black handbag over her shoulder and skips down the front steps and into a waiting taxi.

'*Hasta mañana*,' she shouts, raising her hand in a casual wave to the young man who has taken over for the morning.

'*Hasta mañana*,' he shouts back.

The hotel settles into an easy silence for a second time, with only the occasional guest strolling through its front doors. But the big brass clock hanging on the wood-panelled wall is ticking towards 10h00 and still there's no sign of Malema.

The waiter fills my cup with another black coffee as I flick through yesterday's copy of *El Universal*, which blatantly hacks away at the thin shred of credibility that remains of Hugo Chávez's so-called Socialism of the Twenty-first Century.

Splashed across its front page is the news that Venezuela has agreed to repay its US$20 billion loan from China with 100 000 barrels of oil a day for the next ten years. There's talk elsewhere in the paper about how the public sector wage bill is ballooning. And how the bolivar, the local currency, is on a serious slide against the greenback, the next best thing to official tender in the South American country. Inflation is soaring. Rolling power cuts are on the rise. Venezuelans now account for the second-largest number of Latin American exiles in the United States.

Little wonder, says Jorge Urosa Savino, the cardinal of the Catholic Church in Venezuela. On an inside page, the clergyman reminds his followers that 18 April 1810 was the date that marked the beginning of independence from Spain, but what was fought for has been forsaken for Marxist socialism, which does no one any good, he says, and he appeals to the Virgin of Coromoto to protect his country from 'dictatorships, totalitarianism and violence'.

El Comandante appears to be taking it all in his stride, however. He is in the Bolivian city of Cochabamba, where he's attending a conference on climate change, and it seems he went off on a

tangent yesterday to remind his followers that 22 April was the day when Vladimir Lenin was born, in 1870. A man forever to be remembered. *Viva la revolución!*

There are a few short stories about the upcoming FIFA World Cup in South Africa. Venezuela hasn't qualified, but they beat Honduras, which has, in an impressive friendly game on Thursday night. The paper dubs it a 'win at World Cup level'. There's some talk about Bafana Bafana's draw against North Korea. But no mention of the South African renegade youth leader's visit to the country.

Malema only arrived in Venezuela on Thursday morning but he is already bailing out tonight, ahead of time. He has decided to cut short the week-long trip in an all-out effort to put a stop to the disciplinary charges that are hanging over his head back home in South Africa.

The executive of the ANC will meet on Monday to discuss the political fate of Malema, whose public behaviour has gone from woeful to wicked ever since he became president of the ANC Youth League (ANCYL) in April 2008. In all that time, and for reasons known only to themselves, the ANC leaders have tended to turn a blind eye and deaf ear to the young man's controversial style of politics. Even the prominent men and women in the ranks of the party, people who were once fearless in the face of the brutal apartheid regime during the struggle era, opted for silence when Malema was at his worst; when he was inviting shame on the party and the country, trousering his fair share of public tenders and instilling confusion and fear in many ordinary South Africans, most of whom had arrived at the dismaying conclusion that Malema was untouchable.

But the patience of the senior ANC leadership finally snapped a couple of weeks back when the twenty-nine-year-old

began to lose the run of himself on a number of fronts. Within a few weeks of his trotting out the old struggle song 'Shoot the Boer', the country's most notorious Boer, Eugene Terre'Blanche, was murdered on his farm in North West province. The day he was killed, Easter Saturday, Malema was singing high praises for President Robert Mugabe in Harare at a time when South Africa was supposedly acting as a neutral broker, trying to keep the fragile peace put in place by the year-old unity government. Then, a few days later, Malema made a fine international spectacle of himself when he hurled some extraordinary verbal abuse at a journalist at a televised press conference as the whole world looked on. That was the day he earned himself the nickname Kidi Amin. And to top it all off, he then compared President Jacob Zuma to his predecessor, Thabo Mbeki. Benign though the comparison was, it touched a raw nerve in the incumbent.

That's when the ANC finally began to move towards disciplinary measures to try to deal with the youth, something that is not customary practice for the party and which it has done only a handful of times in its 100-year history. Monday will decide just how far the leadership is intending to go this time.

'And if I'm not there, I don't exist,' Malema says.

His only option is to take the overnight flight from Caracas to São Paulo tonight, spend the day in the sprawling Brazilian city tomorrow and take the overnight connection to Johannesburg on Sunday, touching down at O.R. Tambo International Airport on Monday morning about an hour ahead of the scheduled start of the meeting.

The only reason I'm here is to gather information for this book, and I've changed my tickets so that I can travel back with him, and there's little point in my leaving the hotel until I know what his movements are for the day.

The lift is out of order and I see him shuffling down the narrow stairwell a short while later, his bodyguard trotting two steps behind him. Malema's face is like thunder and though he is no towering giant in any physical sense – standing tall at just shy of 1.65 metres – his negative energy appears to sap the sunlit room of its gaiety.

I tell him that the bus has left without him, though I suspect he already knows that.

'I'm not going to that thing,' he says in a low growl, flicking his hand dismissively as he lowers himself into the armchair next to mine.

That 'thing' is the conference of the World Federation of Democratic Youth taking place in downtown Caracas this week. Malema has led a delegation of more than a dozen South Africans to the meeting, among them young men and women from the ANCYL, the Young Communist League, the Pan Africanist Congress, the South African Students Congress and the Congress of South African Students. South Africa is scheduled to host the World Festival of Youth and Students in Soweto at the end of this year, 2010, and the delegation has travelled here to pick up the baton. Malema did that yesterday at the city hall.

The conference will wrap up today, but it seems he won't be there when it does. It's not a big deal. He has already fulfilled his official duties. And besides, Chávez is not here to meet him anyway, contrary to what Malema was led to believe.

So he has decided to bow out and focus his mind instead on his political future back home on the far side of the Atlantic, more than ten thousand kilometres away. Small talk is not coming easily this morning.

President Zuma had a meeting last night with Fikile Mbalula about the disciplinary move. Mbalula was the president of the

ANCYL before Malema took over the post, and he then went on to become a cabinet minister in Zuma's government as well as a rising strongman in the ANC. Throughout it all, he has remained a close friend and political ally of Malema's. On the eve of the departure to Venezuela, Zuma had requested a private meeting with Malema himself. And as much as Malema wanted and needed that man-to-man talk, he simply couldn't agree to it with one foot already on the plane to Caracas. So he sent his right-hand man along instead to try to talk the president down.

He gives me the thumbs up when I ask how it went, though he refuses to utter a word. His gesture would suggest the outcome was positive, or relatively so, yet he's looking awfully bothered.

In his mind, I guess, it is Monday morning, not Saturday morning. And already he is in Albert Luthuli House in downtown Johannesburg, not here in Hotel Avila in the Venezuelan capital.

In fairness to Malema, it's hard to read the situation. His enemies have been crawling out of the woodwork this past week or so, gathering behind the pending charges, and he's still not sure who is with him and who is against him in that 86-member national executive committee (NEC) of the ANC. Even in the ranks of its Youth League, he can no longer count on the support of some of his own.

Last Monday, the League's top leaders met their seniors in the ANC to plead their case and argue why Malema shouldn't be taken to task. On Tuesday, some of the country's main newspapers carried front-page stories stating that the charges had been dropped, only for the ANC to call a press conference later that morning to tell the media otherwise. The charges hadn't been dropped at all. Someone was playing a tricky game by forcing the hand of the ANC leadership in the way that they did.

'Why did you tell me the charges were dropped when they weren't?' one journalist asked what he thought was his ANCYL source over the phone just minutes after the press conference ended that morning.

But the journalist had unwittingly dialled the wrong number. Not only that, but he had identified himself by name at the top of the conversation and also revealed the identity of his source to the listener on the other end of the line when he uttered his name in a greeting. He only realised his mistake when the listener identified himself, a man who bears the same first name as the source the journalist thought he was calling.

To make matters worse, he was speaking to someone who immediately picked up the phone to Malema and relayed the story in full, who then knew that at least one of his own leaders was working against him, leaking misleading information to the press.

Malema has no idea how many more are busy plotting against him while he's here in South America and this is also virgin territory for him. He has been getting away with blue murder for so long but it looks as if it could all come crashing down at any time now. So I opt to keep the conversation light.

'Where's the Breitling?' I ask, when I notice that the wristwatch he's wearing is not the expensive, flashy-looking one that is usually featured in photos of him in the press.

'It's broken,' he tells me, again waving his hand in that characteristic dismissive gesture of his, his face still set in a firm frown.

I ask what happened to it and he launches into the sorry tale.

The watch, which was from the exclusive Breitling for Bentley range, met its demise late in 2009, roughly around the same time

as the Malema brand began to fray within the ranks of the ANC. It happened one afternoon when he was spending some time with his son Ratanang, his only child, at his home in Polokwane.

Ratanang was a big fan of *Ben 10*, the American animation series about young Ben Tennyson and his watch-like device with its supernatural powers that allow the young boy to transform into alien characters, and to three-year-old Ratanang, Dad's flashy Breitling looked just like Ben's extraordinary watch.

'Can I play with it?' he asked.

'You can,' his father answered as he unstrapped the wristwatch and handed it to the child.

Ratanang began to fiddle with the dials of the watch, just like Ben does. He imagined himself programming it with the DNA of the alien he was about to transform into. Then, as he had seen Ben do a thousand times, he swiftly raised his little arm upwards, as if he were getting ready for take-off into some other world, and that's when the big Breitling slid off his small wrist and soared into the air before falling flat on the floor seconds later.

With the thud, the Breitling signature gold wings became detached from the top of the face of the watch and were left swivelling beneath the glass.

The child could still hear the tick-tock of the watch and he could see that the second hand was still in motion, but the gold wings were out of place and one look at his father's thunderous face told him he had done something terribly wrong.

He continued to look at him, but he had no words to match his father's stare. So the pair just looked at one another in silence.

The watch was not beyond repair, but in one small innocent act the young boy had damaged one of his father's most distinguished symbols of status and wealth. And that was the end of the Breitling Bentley.

I can picture it all so vividly. I can see that look of rage on Malema's face. I can imagine the child wilting in front of his angry father. And I can't speak for laughter as the story comes to an end.

'It's OK,' Malema says, in an attempt to dismiss my laughter suggesting it was no big deal. It was nothing that money couldn't put right anyway, which he duly did in the weeks that followed, adding to his impressive watch collection, which by now is worth a fair penny.

'I bought another one,' he says as he unstraps the watch he is wearing and hands it to me.

It's a very nice watch and I tell him so. But it's not a Breitling and I wonder why he didn't replace it with one from the same brand.

'No, I did. This is just another one,' he says. 'I have many watches. Many, many watches, to match my shoes.'

'Why to match your shoes?' I want to know.

'Fiona,' he goads, looking at me with an expression that is heaped with scorn, pity and dismay all rolled into one.

'The leather in your shoes is supposed to match the leather in your belt and your watch. So if you wear brown leather shoes,' he tells me, as he points to his soft, brown leather Yves Saint Laurent slip-ons, 'you must wear a brown leather belt,' he continues, tugging at the waist of his trousers, 'and a brown leather watch,' tapping on his left wrist with his right forefinger in a confident gesture, happy now that he has the upper hand in the conversation.

The heavy mood of a few minutes ago is now long gone.

This is the young South African who preaches on behalf of the poor and to the poor, the man who promises to bring on the next stage of the so-called National Democratic Revolution in South

Africa; and here he is in Hugo Chávez's Venezuela lecturing on the finer points of fashion.

'Far from coordinated leather you were reared,' I remind him.

'That's the way it is,' he replies.

'Who taught you all of this?' I want to know. And why would he care to abide by it all, he who shows scant respect for any kind of rule or reason at the best of times?

'You don't know what you are talking about,' he responds. 'Look at you.'

Venezuela has never seen so many designer labels as it has these past forty-eight hours since the arrival of the South African young ones. They descended on the city with their expensive suitcases and travel bags, top-of-the-range baseball caps, flashy T-shirts, snazzy shoes and sneakers, sleek manbags and a string of other expensive accessories hanging out of them – and a bodyguard in tow – all dressed up for a socialist youth conference.

I have been wondering how they must appear in the eyes of the other youth who have flown in from all over the world and who are also staying at the Avila. The three-star hotel is swarming with casually dressed, young delegates and among them, to my mind at least, the South Africans seem to stand out a mile. They are misfits in this mix. They look as if they don't belong. Some of them look more like mafia than young militant activists. But the look on Malema's face suggests that it is I who has been conspicuous all this while, among the South Africans at least, and I appear to have let the side down badly.

I'm not wearing a belt or a watch, but the problem seems to be with my red patent, open sandals and black-and-brown leather bag.

'What's wrong with me?' I ask.

By now curiosity has crept up on the receptionist as he fixes his look in our direction. I'm not sure that he speaks English well enough to understand fully what is being said, but he seems to be getting the gist of Malema's body language.

'Your shoes are not the right colour for your bag,' Malema tells me, pointing to my feet. 'They should be matching. They should be the same.'

'Who said?' I ask again.

Malema's hometown friend, Patti Nkobe, tells me she suspects that his friend Fana Hlongwane, of the multibillion-rand arms deal fame, advises Malema on his style (as she claims he does on everything else). But if he does, Malema is not letting on.

'That's fashion, man,' he tells me. 'I know.'

The conversation is only getting going when a young American man brings it to a halt.

'Are you Julius Malema?' he asks in a broad North American twang.

'No,' Malema answers with brazen mendacity, as he looks the other way.

'Are you sure you are not Julius Malema from the African National Congress in South Africa?' the man asks for a second time, before explaining that he is a locally based journalist who has been asked by South Africa's *Sunday Times* to try to track Malema down in Venezuela to find out what he is up to.

'No, no. Sesotho. Sesotho,' Malema says, suggesting he can only speak in his mother tongue as he tries to confuse and discourage the journalist.

'Oh, you are from Lesotho. Oh, I'm sorry,' he says as he takes a few steps back, the look on his face suggesting he is not entirely convinced that this is not his subject, though he's not about to challenge the sullen-looking character either.

'Yes,' Malema grunts.

The journalist turns on his heel and begins to walk slowly towards the front doors. But within seconds, he turns around and marches towards Malema, his hand outstretched as he holds up the mirror image of the Youth League leader that he has cleverly sourced on his cellphone. The young man sitting in front of him, decked out in designer regalia from head to toe, couldn't be anyone but the South African youth he is supposed to be tailing.

'Are you sure you are not Julius Malema?' he ventures again with a broad smile on his face as he holds up the phone for Malema to see.

Malema breaks into his mother tongue for a second time and he rants on for a minute or two, gesticulating with his hands and flicking his wrists as he always does when he gets hot under the collar. He then stands up and hails a taxi and stomps out of the hotel, leaving the journalist looking bewildered in his wake.

2010 is turning out to be a black year for Malema and the world is closing in on him. Not even here, on the other side of the world, can he escape the pressures that are weighing on him back home.

Chapter 3

The making of Malema

If anything, 2010 turned out to be Julius Malema's *annus horribilis*, the year when he was forced to face the sobering truth that his popularity within the ANC had waned, that his leash would never be so long again. Henceforth, he would have to fight for his political survival and secure his clout by other means, neither of which was beyond him.

It was a frustrating how-do-you-do for a man who had inhabited a political paradise ever since he took over the presidency of the ANCYL, by which time the ANC was already ripe for the picking for a man of Malema's calibre and ambition. Outwardly the ANC was a giant force resting on the overwhelming majority of support from the country's twenty-million-strong electorate, but it was the internecine rivalry within its ranks that was tearing it apart. The tensions pre-dated the Malema era and went as far back as 1990 when the party was unbanned, and that was the great irony: during its thirty years as an underground movement, with its leadership in exile and its members scattered throughout South Africa and all over the world, the former liberation movement held together better than it ever did in the early years of the democratic dispensation that they would put in place and ultimately govern.

Of course, that had everything to do with the common enemy it had in the apartheid regime and which it eventually helped bring down. Yet, though the ANC could dote on its past achievements as a liberation movement, it struggled to cover itself in glory as a ruling party, and instead of the revolutionary tradition giving way to the people-centred democracy it clearly promised in those early months, the ANC became a self-serving organisation instead.

Naturally the competing factions were quick to surface, even long before Nelson Mandela stepped down in 1999, but they became more aggressive under Thabo Mbeki's stewardship that followed. There was a time when Mbeki was South Africa's great hope. A well-educated man, he had a good grasp of the intricacies of an emerging nation that was still socially defined by centuries of white domination. He also had a clear vision of what he wanted South Africa to become.

Mbeki was also an aloof sort, however, with a healthy authoritarian streak coursing through his veins, and it was the distance he manifested between himself and 'his people' that eventually led to his demise.

Zuma had been Mbeki's deputy, both at the party and state level, but he was dropped from government halfway through 2005 when he was implicated in a massive corruption scandal. The move was quick to backfire, though, when a not insignificant number of Mbeki's critics within the ANC used it as an opportunity to bring him down instead, eventually ousting him as party president two years later.

Rather than unite the party, as Zuma had promised in his comeback campaign, the ANC began to fracture even further under the new leadership that was put in place at the landmark

conference in Polokwane late in 2007 and only a fool would have been blind to the opportunities the new milieu presented.

Though Malema was only in his mid-twenties at the time and a budding leader in the Youth League, he was one of the key people who pushed for Zuma's return. His pickings were rich, to begin with at least, and doors soon began to swing open for him in all directions. His lap was laden with largesse, he was cut into big business deals and he was drawn close to the party's decision-making table, all of which came with the terrain of ANC power. Within a few months of Zuma taking the presidency of the ANC, Malema became his junior partner when he was elected president of the Youth League, and for Malema it was like a windfall.

One can't help but wonder what might have been if the ANC had been more united or perhaps better guided in those years, or were the likes of Malema simply going to float to the surface anyway in country as divided as South Africa is.

Though it was not a personal friendship that bound them, politically Malema and Zuma were as thick as thieves to begin with and they would have defended one another to the death, despite their forty-year age gap. They were also quite similar in character. There was something brutish and crude, if not mean, about them both and their louche behaviour. Though they both had the thinnest of political skins, neither man was lacking in guile nor did they care a whit for the good of the country. Their sole concern was power, something that Zuma would eventually struggle to maintain.

During his first year as party leader, Zuma was insecure and weighed down by the corruption scandals he was fighting in the courts. His apprehension was understandable as the charges were damning enough to have him put behind bars.

Yet even though they were mysteriously dropped on the eve of the general elections in 2009 that made him state president, he still never managed to find a steady footing in the years that followed. His first year in office was rocked by the scandal of a love child that he fathered with Irvin Khosa's daughter, adding to the twenty-plus children he already had from his polygamous marriages and extramarital affairs. Allegations of corruption and fraud continued to hound him, his family and close friends. In those first few years the country weathered some of the most awful scandals, not least the Marikana massacre and the multi-million-rand Nkandla shame. Zuma had packed his cabinet with cronies and they too began to pluck from the public purse. Never was the Public Protector so busy as during the 2009–2014 period when she probed one wrongdoing after another, with little or no significant impact.

The Zuma era also marked a fairly radical shift in government planning, yet he didn't seem to grasp the complexity of it all. He was and remains inarticulate on his own policy and it was hard to understand what the toneless leader ever really stood for or where his legacy would eventually lie. Of course he had his strengths and there were moments of greatness, but there were more times when he appeared to be an apology away from a presidential demise. From the day he was sworn into office, his mind was focused on one thing and one thing only: staying there and away from the glare of the judiciary that still wanted to pore over his past financial affairs, while ensuring his financial future remained bright.

On the whole Zuma was unfit for the purpose of leading South Africa and I suspect he knew as much. Like any feeble leader would in such circumstances, he developed a deep sense of paranoia. During the struggle against apartheid, he had been

a spy chief for the ANC and that began to show during his first term as state president. Adamant to control the climate and keep the various forces at bay, he manipulated state security structures to keep an eye on those around him. He dared not appoint any degree of excellence to his team, lest they outshine him; hence it was not too long before he began to amass an army of enemies both at government and party level. Malema was chief among them.

Despite the similarities between the two of them, there was one crucial thing that set them apart: Malema had the kind of political skill that Zuma could only dream about. He was one of what cartoonist Zapiro called the 'Pirates of Polokwane' and he was fast becoming the most vocal of this new breed. The sun had not long set over the Polokwane conference when it became apparent that he was the more astute among them as well. In his early days as president of the Youth League he began to cash in on one of Zuma's biggest failings: the neglect of the masses, the tens of millions of poor South Africans who are the single biggest and most important constituency in the country by a very long shot.

Zuma had lobbied them aggressively in his comeback campaign, but he was quick to turn his back on them as soon as he got into office and became one of the new elite himself. And though Malema had also found firm footing among the upper echelons, he knew better than to turn his back on the core of South African society and in a clever move he began to play a cunning double game: he promised the masses all sorts of everything that they wanted to hear, starting with the spreading of the country's wealth and the nationalisation of the trillion-dollar mines. He then turned to the thorny and emotive issue of the land and threatened to imitate Mugabe's style of 'land grabbing' if need

be. Whatever it was they wanted, or what he would tell them they wanted, he promised he would make happen.

Only very few among the underclass questioned Malema's sincerity. It was common knowledge that he was a young man of conspicuous wealth, yet they seemed to allow him the contradiction and so with remarkable ease and little effort, his national profile began to grow as he became a locomotive force among the masses.

He was a young political genius, but it was an adage that few were willing to grant him then. In 2008 he was also a notorious populist in the eyes of most, the kind of figure who bodes no good. A malicious genius was perhaps the more fitting title.

He was becoming an extraordinary phenomenon, wiping the floor with his party peers and seniors. But while as a political strategist he showed brilliance, he lacked discretion where it mattered most. He enjoyed a lavish lifestyle that begged understandable scrutiny. At the beginning of 2010 he was netting a monthly salary from the ruling party that should have placed him in the bracket of middle-income earners, yet he lived a life that befitted a man of far greater wealth. He had developed an approach to business through politics that linked his name to a string of shady business deals on the back of a multitude of public tenders that began to raise questions around what was beginning to look like a lack of muscular integrity on his part. Amid allegations of corruption and fears that his business interests might not withstand the scrutiny of the taxman, a number of public investigations were started into his financial and business affairs.

It was all too much for the ruling party. Malema was drawing too much attention to the dark side of their politics. He was not the first to become conspicuously wealthy in their name, and he

wouldn't be the last of them to feed off the fiscus, but a focus on his excesses would surely extend to other party members and the system of patronage that had become commonplace.

Malema was also rising too fast in the eyes of many of his party seniors. The ANC's planning in terms of succession was – and remains – lacking. The Polokwane conference had exposed that much. But if Malema were to continue rising at the pace he was going, he could easily wipe out a generation of cadres who had been patiently and diligently working their way through the ranks.

Even among his friends and close political allies the competition became fierce, often in a way that would jolt Malema. Though he was enjoying every moment of his political fame, there was no one more taken aback by it all than Malema himself, yet it was his close friend Fikile Mbalula who attempted to halt him in his tracks early on. Late one night when they both had had a few to drink, Mbalula turned to him and said: 'You can't become president before me, man. I have to become president first. Then you. But not you first.'

Many a true word is spoken in jest, and many a drunk man's words are the sober man's thoughts. But were the power games within the ANC *really* so frivolous around that time? Whatever the case, Malema was evidently perceived as a threat within the party but he was also becoming an embarrassment to the party itself. There was the unforgettable trip to Harare in the Easter of 2010, followed by the clash with the BBC journalist upon his return to Luthuli House, and he was finally slapped down with a heavy warning.

Looking back over newspaper clippings and reports from that time, it is incredible the extent to which that early disciplinary move was covered by the media, a testament, no

doubt, to Malema's enormous profile by then. He was, after all, only the leader of the ruling party's youth wing though he had outstepped that station a long time back.

In hindsight, disciplining him proved to be an ill-considered notion that reflected more negatively on the ANC than on Malema himself. In an ideal world, he should have been challenged in a thorough and internal political debate or taught that a party puts policy in place for good reason. But Zuma's ANC lacked the leadership to see that through. It had become an organisation of factions, one of which Malema belonged to. And the contours of each faction had begun to blur, which made the task of challenging him all the more difficult – hence the call for a harsh disciplinary hearing.

'We needed to see who was behind Malema,' one member of the ANC's executive told me around that time. 'We knew that a lot of the senior comrades were with him, but we didn't know for sure. And the only way to find out would be to discipline him and see who would come to his defence. And it worked. We saw it clearly.'

It had come to that. The ruling ANC had fractured to the extent that the left hand didn't know quite what the right hand was doing at the executive level.

After weeks of agonising threats and strategically leaked reports and grim predictions, Malema was finally handed a paltry suspended sentence in May. He was also instructed to apologise for his behaviour and asked to attend anger management classes, as well as make a donation to a charity of his choice, all of which he ignored. He appeared every bit the political outcast set to become a thing of the past and the media rushed to write his obituary. But it was a statement of political death that was written in haste, because a year to the day after I had sat with

him in that hotel foyer in Caracas, Malema was revelling in his new-found status.

He had become a political hero as the villain in a hate speech trial that was initiated by AfriForum over his singing of the struggle song '*Dubula iBhunu*' ('Shoot the Boer'), and it was a court case that played right into his lap.

Like his political forebears, Malema finally had his day in court. It was an important moment for him and one that would give him the political legitimacy he lacked because the court plays a pivotal role in ANC struggle and contemporary history. Until then he had no 'struggle credentials', as ANC types are wont to say. He was born in the latter years of the apartheid regime and was therefore too young to have served in exile, in the ANC trenches within the country, or behind bars in a South African jail. He traded instead on the fact that his mother had been a domestic worker, something that is commonly flagged by many black South Africans to exemplify their wrongful place of servitude to fellow whites. But now Malema was about to earn his stripes, within the confines of a Johannesburg courtroom.

Nelson Mandela, Walter Sisulu, Ahmed Kathrada, Govan Mbeki and a number of other 'greats' of the struggle era had come to prominence during the Rivonia Trial in the early 1960s when they were tried, though not convicted, for treason (though they were given life sentences for sabotage) in what became one of the most high-profile cases of the apartheid era. In taking on the white judiciary they had become martyrs in the eyes of the masses at a difficult moment in black South African history.

Zuma also had his day in court during a controversial rape trial that ironically made him a man of the people while he was still deputy president of the country (though it was by evading a second court case in 2009 on corruption charges that he came to power).

Then along came Malema and as a prominent young blade he strode into the courtroom each day of that week-long trial with Madikizela-Mandela on his arm, the pair of them flanked by a small army of security guards wielding large machine guns in a stomach-churning spectacle intended to allow him to defend his militancy in peacetime South Africa.

Yet he handled himself impeccably when he took the stand (save for one hitch when he put the starting year of apartheid in the mid-1960s instead of 1948). His tone was calm and his argument was coherent and not once did he allow his cage to be rattled, though he was afforded ample opportunity to vent some rage.

'I belong to a militant and very radical organisation and if you are not militant, you run the risk of being irrelevant,' Malema told the court. 'We are heroes. Yes, we are warriors because we won war battles.'

He was bent on becoming a powerhouse politician and he was showing few signs of defeat that April. The only chink in his armour was a physical one, however. Malema was suffering from gout and it hits him 'always after we have been drinking a lot and eating a lot of meat,' he had once told me. But it hit him hard at the courthouse during one particularly long and drawn-out period of cross-examination. He was on the stand, though he was seated, and he forced himself to his feet to try to relieve the pain in his legs. He was mid-spiel at the time, talking up the revolution, when the pain worsened, but he didn't flinch. And it was an unforgettable portrait: the so-called commander-in-chief of economic freedom, defending the ANC's war songs while fighting off the self-inflicted rich man's disease of gout.

In defending himself in that very high-profile trial, Malema became not only the custodian of ANC struggle songs, but a hero

in the eyes of millions, and within a very short period of time he was back in the hive of political action.

It gave him an extraordinary boost and it came at an extraordinary time. He was facing a re-election for the presidency of the ANCYL shortly after and despite the popular image portrayed of him during that trial, Malema had his fair share of detractors within the ranks of the Youth League by then. During his first term as president he had developed an intolerant and dictatorial style of rule. Those who weren't with him were against him and were duly ousted from the party's ranks. Hence, by the time the ANCYL conference was pencilled in for June 2011, there was an army of opponents who were preparing to take him on, rallying behind Lebogang Maile, the chairman of the League in Gauteng, who would challenge Malema for the position of president.

Malema's court days made Maile's challenge all the more difficult. For many, Malema had become much more than a leader of the youth. He was a man of the people now, the 'boy brave' of the country's suffering classes and finally ranked among his forebears.

It all coincided with the campaign for the local government elections of May 2011 and Malema hit the campaign trail early on, knowing it would provide him with the platform he was looking for. He had a profile to build and the publicity he was about to earn from his court appearance would go a long way. What was foremost on his mind, however, was not necessarily the pending Youth League conference but the ANC's next round of leadership elections that would take place at the end of 2012. Only five years had passed since Malema had helped secure the party presidency for Zuma, but his desire now was to unseat him so that he could continue his march towards greater power.

The local elections marked a shift in the thinking of the regular voters who for years had voted with their hearts, based on the emotional attachment that so many had had to the ANC which had overturned the franchise to include blacks in 1994. But now the electorate was looking for results and if the ANC couldn't provide them, they would begin to look elsewhere. So Malema appealed to them with an extraordinary charm and talked to the masses in a way that no other politician did on that campaign trail that year. Not even Zuma.

Malema stole the show and he, more than Zuma, became the face of the ANC during that month-long campaign. He even had many of the media onside. They clapped him warmly on the back for a job well done, and there was not a whisper of the controversies they had been peddling not too long before then. A month later he secured himself a second term as ANCYL president, by which time his chest was well and truly protruding with pride.

It was a remarkable turn of events in the space of twelve months. Malema had come back against all the odds and despite enormous hostility. If ever he appeared unstoppable, it was then.

But lurking beneath that brash veneer was a host of dark secrets about his moneymaking activities, which not even he could defend, and details of which began to leak all over the country's newspapers in the weeks that followed. Not surprisingly, it sparked the interest of the authorities, many of which had already been focused on his finances for a long time anyway.

It had little effect on Malema, though. He simply continued to up his political game against the ANC leadership in the bold and brazen way that only he knew best. In one instance he called for regime change in neighbouring Botswana, contrary to ANC

and South African foreign policy, and in a desperate move, the ruling party slapped him with disciplinary charges for a second time. Of course he knew he was courting trouble, but he did not anticipate it would knock on his door the day that it did.

It was the last Friday in August 2011 and I had spoken to him by phone early that morning. The first edition of this book was due to hit the shelves the following week and he had asked to see a copy of it before it did, which the publishers and I had agreed to. Before he made his way to the ANC's executive meeting that morning, he called me to make arrangements to meet at his Sandton home after his day was done. But as soon as he took his seat at the meeting, he was told that the leadership had decided to move against him for a second time.

Though he had escaped relatively unharmed a year earlier, he knew he would not be so lucky this time round and two months later he was slapped with a suspended sentence. He chose to appeal it but the new year brought no reprieve; the five-year suspension he was handed in November 2011 turned to a full expulsion on the leap day of 2012. Of course, Malema also challenged that but he was eventually forced to part ways with the ANC on 24 April.

He would not have felt it then, but that move was the making of Malema. He may have been 'a scratch on the minds' of many South Africans, to borrow Harold Isaacs's words, yet there was nothing craven about his following among the masses and he knew as much. As he gave a parting look to his peers, the million and more men and women who pledged allegiance to the ANC, he knew there wasn't a handful among them possessed with the extraordinary gravitas he was.

Chapter 4

Do you know who I am?

Julius Malema's early life story explains much about the kind of man he was to become, though his upbringing was really no different to that of millions of other South African men and women of his generation, and indeed other generations before and after. Yet he remains fairly guarded about his family life and is particularly chary about his grandmother Sarah.

The old woman, now in her nineties, is the matriarch of a family that, years ago, was unheard of in South African history but which, by virtue of her famous grandson, has now made its way into the public record. In an unprecedented move, Malema allowed me to meet Sarah at her home, in the township of Seshego, one Saturday morning in 2010 so that she could sketch out the family history, first-hand.

In the late 1940s, Mohanwa Johannes Malema met Mathebu Sarah Thobakgale in what was then called the northern region of the Transvaal. She was born in the town of Louis Trichardt and he was from the Batlokwa region. She was also much younger than him, some sixteen years his junior. But he was a widower and he wasn't about to throw away his second chance at happiness because of his new lady friend's age, and shortly after their paths crossed he took her hand in marriage and they settled down and

worked as farmhands not far from the village of Ga-Ramokgopa, where he came from.

Ga-Ramokgopa is a low-lying settlement located about five hundred metres off the N1, the highway that cuts through the country in a diagonal direction, from the Western Cape in the south-west through to Limpopo's border crossing with Zimbabwe in the north-east, forming the first leg of the Cape-to-Cairo highway.

But it is also a desolate part of the world that throws up few opportunities for a man to make a go of his life and if Johannes Malema was to father a new family and fend for them, he knew he would have to try his luck at finding a job in the city of Pietersburg, what is today known as Polokwane, some sixty-odd kilometres south.

He did as most other men had done before him and went ahead of his new wife in search of work. He headed straight for New Pietersburg, the industrial stretch to the west of the city, and within a few weeks he found a job at the local cement factory and a place to lay his head at night in nearby Disteneng.

Disteneng had originally been developed on a large swathe of land cleared for the workers who serviced New Pietersburg, or for men who were travelling from the bantustans or far afield and for whom transport was a problem. But it instantly became an area attractive to squatters and in an all-out bid to put a halt to that, the earlier settlers were given the opportunity to buy out the small plots of land on which they then built their homes; hence the name Disteneng, the Sepedi word for 'stand owners'. Over the years, Disteneng developed into a densely populated, multiracial settlement that was home to Africans, Indians and coloureds (that awful apartheid racial categorisation that has carried into the new South Africa).

On each stand stood a small house with a tin shack, if not two or three, in its backyard and it was into one of those tumbledown

dwellings that the Malemas moved when Johannes sent for Sarah and their firstborn, Maropeng.

But they were a pitiful lot. Though they had a wage coming in, it was hardly worth talking about, and the family was ballooning. After Maropeng was born, five other children followed in quick succession: Philemon, Florah, Nurse, Annie and Francina. And with so many mouths to feed, it was often the case that they didn't have two pennies to rub together at the end of each week.

In the 1960s the white government decided to break up the multiracial block in Disteneng and forcibly removed the dwellers to three different areas. The Africans were relocated further out to the north-west of the city to the new township of Seshego, named after the King of Moletjie. In those early days, Seshego was also the capital of the Lebowa bantustan until the chief minister, Dr Cedric Phatudi, relocated the seat of government to his home village of Ga-Mphahlele in the early 1970s. The Indians were moved closer to the city to the suburb of Nirvana, while the coloureds were relocated to Westenberg to the west of the city centre.

The shack dwellers of Disteneng were the first targets of forced removal, on the assumption that they would put up least resistance with the offer of a house that they could call home, and that is how the Malema family got the first permanent roof over their heads when, in 1964, they were allocated house number 1103 in what was called Zone 1. Seven other zones followed to make up Seshego, but Zone 1 was where the first cluster of houses was erected and house 1103 was on the street where the first strip of bungalows was unveiled.

Zone 1 was a large area made up of hundreds and hundreds of homes and it was subsequently broken down into five sub-sections by the people who lived there. They gave each sub-area

an informal name that had resonance for them and which has stuck to this day.

Groovy, for example, took its name from the first soccer club that was formed in that area. A big marula tree in a nearby section gave Moruleng its name. Each house had at least four numbers that determined its address, and those that began with the digits 12 fell into what became known as the Di 12 section and, by the same logic, those that began with the numbers 15 fell into the Di 15 cluster.

The section where the Malemas lived was called Masakaneng, the Sepedi word for 'sacks', because that was what the residents covered the windows of their new homes with. Curtains were a luxury then. For people who had known nothing other than shack life, so too were the windows, if not the houses as well. And the best they had to drape over the apertures were the sacks from mealie meal, or maize, the staple food of the South African diet, then and now.

'Masakaneng was a name that was taken from Disteneng,' says Thabo Makunyane, the former executive mayor of Polokwane. 'The sacks were made from hemp. And we used to use the sacks and cardboard and anything else we could get our hands on to make *mukhukhu* [shacks],' he remembers. 'And when we moved to Seshego, that name came with us.'

'The people of Masakaneng had nothing, nothing,' says Matlala Maremane, a man who was born in the 1960s in that stretch of the township. 'It was the poorest of the poor who lived there. And it was the worst part of Seshego, with every bad element to be expected of a run-down area like that. I know. I grew up there.'

'I remember there were no street lights,' says Freddie Ramaphakela, who was also reared in Zone 1. 'And it was dangerous to go out at night. Even by day, the area wasn't safe.'

It was in Masakaneng that the Malemas spent the rest of their days. Theirs was a four-roomed house, comprising two bedrooms, a living-room-cum-dining-room and a kitchen. In the yard outside stood the toilet that fed into a substandard sewerage system. House 1103 had running water, but no electricity. But that was their lot, for which they paid just over R2 each month in rent.

As a family they struggled. Sarah found it hard to make ends meet on Johannes's income, which was not always regular. And her family was still growing. After they moved to Seshego, she had three more children: Maria, Anna and Martha.

Then the grandchildren began to appear and the household numbers began to swell. With the exception of Maropeng, who left home when she got married in 1971, and Annie, who left home in 1986, the rest of the Malema daughters, as well as Philemon, stayed at home. Anna and Martha did not have children. Philemon did but the child was reared by the mother elsewhere. Altogether, Florah, Francina, Nurse and Maria had nine children out of wedlock, all of whom were reared in house 1103 (though two of Florah's children died in infancy).

One day in the early 1970s, Johannes walked out on his family when he met another woman, leaving Sarah to rear the largely female household on her own.

'But we were no different to many others,' Sarah says.

She was a traditional healer and a believer and put her faith in the gods and her ancestors to help see her and her family through, but the best years of her life were marred by one form of hardship after another.

Philemon, who became the main breadwinner after Johannes left, had a nervous breakdown and was forced to give up work. Florah, Sarah's third child and Julius's mother, was in Standard 6

(now known as Grade 8) when she was diagnosed with epilepsy. She was in her late teens when the doctors explained her condition to her and she was forced to abandon her schooling.

By then Sarah was really struggling with the single-headed household and was holding down a full-time job in a local mill trying to make ends meet. Seeing the strain it was taking on her mother, Florah decided to find a job to help pay her way. Like the vast majority of black women then, and even now to some extent, Florah, who was known to all around her as Sesi Mahlodi, worked as a domestic helper for a family in the largely Indian suburb of Nirvana, but she continued to live at her Seshego home and covered the distance to and from her workplace each day by mini-bus taxi.

She wasn't long in that job when an epileptic attack crept up on her one day, leaving her maimed for the rest of her life. She was standing over the gas stove in her employers' kitchen when her body went into convulsions. She fainted and as she collapsed she pulled a pot of boiling water on top of her, which instantly licked at the skin on her neck and chest, scorching it into a fine layer.

After a brief stint in hospital, and on the doctor's orders, she was forced to give up her job and never worked another day. She returned home to her mother's house where she lived until 2006, when a severe epileptic seizure overcame her early one morning and she died. It was 14 August and she was fifty years old.

Complicating Florah's life was the fact that she was apparently mentally unstable. Friends and neighbours recall a frail person whom they describe as emotionally challenged, a grown woman who maintained the innocence of a child until the day she died.

The Malema house sits on a T-junction and opposite it stands the Corner Store, a busy hub and hang-out and a magnet for the children of Masakaneng. Florah spent her days stretched out

under the mango tree outside her family's house, watching out for her son who rarely left the streets. She dozed in the shade of the tree throughout the day. And when she wasn't taking a nap, she said little and simply sat and watched the street life unfolding around her. All the children who grew up in Masakaneng knew Florah Malema well.

But her son insists that, mentally, his mother was as normal as the next woman and that any suggestion of emotional instability stems from the social mores that come with epilepsy. Though it is not caused by mental illness and does not result in mental impairment, the condition often carries with it a social stigma because of the unsightly body behaviour a seizure can bring on. The medical books describe it as an abnormal electrical discharge from the brain cells. There is no advance warning. The muscles often go into spasm and the body can become rigid before going into convulsions. The person will lose consciousness and wail and moan as the body goes into fits. Breathing becomes laboured and to see a person in the throes of an epileptic fit is not pleasant by any standards, but in many African cultures it is often regarded as watching a person possessed or truly deranged.

Seeing Florah come out of a seizure, half-dazed and incoherent, was not nice, her son says. It could have been misleading.

Even with the full appreciation of her condition, there is no one who will say a bad word about Florah. She was just another woman who was unlucky in life, through no doing of her own.

Florah was twenty-three when she gave birth to Aida, but the young girl died as a toddler. A couple of years later she fell pregnant again and Julius Sello Malema was born on 3 March 1981, sharing the same birthday as his mother. Julius was two years old when Florah gave birth to her third child, Sarah, who was named after her grandmother. But like Aida, she too died in early childhood.

There are not many photos of Julius's early childhood or of his siblings. There is one of him and one of his sisters, posing with their grandmother. He was too young to remember it being taken, but it is one of his most cherished possessions. There are a couple of others of him, and some more of his mother, but none of him and her together, no enduring visual proof of his immediate family.

That doesn't hinder his memory of his mother or his feelings for her in any way. Julius speaks very fondly of her, and openly so.

'She was always there. Always. And I never had to compete for her affection. It was just me and her,' he says, one small unit in the larger Malema lot.

Florah had a very fiery character, which she got from her father and clearly passed on to her son. And though Julius was the apple of his mother's eye, she was never shy to reprimand him whenever he gave her occasion. Whenever she did, Sarah would come to the young boy's rescue.

So it was that he developed a deep affection for the two women who watched out for him in life. His grandmother understood him and she always stood by him, through thick and thin, both as a young boy and in later life. Though he and his mother didn't always see eye to eye, least of all on his hot-headed outlook on life, their bond was equally solid.

While Julius may be accurately defined by his tough and bullish personality, his eyes brim with emotion when he talks about the morning his mother died and how he fell apart when the paramedics told him they were unable to resuscitate her. He remembers how he had to pull himself together as the head of the household and organise her funeral, and how late one night, many weeks later, the full weight of his mother's death came to

bear when it finally dawned on him that she was not coming back. He cried his fair share of tears that night as that prospect sank in.

He was driving through Polokwane at the time, towards the house he then owned in Flora Park, when it hit him like a bolt out of the blue and his tears came fast and furious.

'I couldn't stop. I was screaming. I had to stop the car and pull over,' he remembers.

He had never known his father. His mother was now dead. And though he knew he could always count on his grandmother, somehow he was on his own in life.

His girlfriend at the time – Maropeng Ramohlale – was heavily pregnant and she gave birth to their son, Ratanang, two months after Florah died. But in that brief period after his mother died and before his son was born, he remembers feeling empty for the first time in his life.

'I had never known emotional pain. Real pain. I had never known death so close.'

But he still had Sarah, a woman he looks up to and who was one of very few able to call the young rebel to order during his heady days in the ANC.

It was she who took him to task when he insulted Naledi Pandor, one of the ANC's senior comrades and then minister of education, during a dispute over student fees early in 2009. Pandor is well spoken and her accent could easily be mistaken for that of a member of England's upper classes, but in trying to take Pandor down a peg, Malema made more of a fool of himself when he said:

'We've got a minister who's using too much time using an American accent without assisting our people. That is the main problem. Let the minister use that fake accent to address our problems and not to behave like a spoilt minister.'

Within a few hours of his unfortunate utterance hitting the headlines, Sarah was confronted twice in Seshego by fellow senior citizens who told her it was not right for her grandson to speak to a senior member of society in such a way. She duly picked up the phone to remind her grandson that he had been reared to respect his elders.

'You will apologise,' she told him.

He did. Though the ANC had called on him to do likewise, it was Sarah's words that echoed loudest in his mind. It was not often she raised a finger but when she did, he knew it was with good reason. He apologised within hours of putting down the phone to her.

'When she talks like that, I listen,' he says.

Yet there is not a whisper of his father. Little is known about the man and his identity is a secret the Malema family appears adamant to keep. Whether this is because he never paid the so-called damage money required in African culture when a woman falls pregnant out of wedlock, or whether it is because neither she nor her family ever wanted to establish a relationship with him, or he with them, is hard to know.

Sarah says she never met him and that only Julius's mother, who is now dead, would have been the appropriate person to talk about him. Julius also claims never to have met his father. Yet his aunt Maropeng says he died a few years back, while neighbours and friends insist Julius's father is well known to all of the Malemas and still lives in Seshego in a shack on the far side of Nelson Mandela Drive that cuts through the township.

But regardless of who he is, he never did and still does not feature in Julius Malema's life; nor does Malema harbour any hopes that he ever will.

'I never had a father in my life,' he says. 'I had my mother and my granny. I didn't know anything else. Why do I need a father? I am a father myself now.'

He was reared as an only child, though he was born into a crowded four-roomed house that was home to his mother, his grandmother, his grandfather for a while, his aunts, an uncle and several cousins.

There was a time when the household numbers swelled to a dozen and more, forcing the Malemas to build two shacks in the backyard to house them all. But what once were shacks are now two double-storey structures that stand tall on that plot in Zone 1, towering over every other house in the immediate vicinity.

At some stage around 2005, when Malema began to make his money, he began to renovate the family home. He wanted to demolish the existing structure and build a bigger and better house in its place, but his grandmother wouldn't hear of it. When Johannes abandoned them years earlier, Sarah had come close to losing that house. It was registered in her husband's name and he wanted to sell it, but she refused and she was forced into a bitter and protracted battle to keep it. She was understandably loathe to entertain her grandson's plans years later when he told her he wanted to raze it to the ground.

'This one is mine,' she told him. 'I fought for it and I'm keeping it.' She would not budge.

He modernised the small house instead. In the backyard he built a two-storey structure, which was just at roofing level when his mother died. And around both houses he had high walls erected and tall gates put in place.

By the time his grandmother entered the evening of her life, and Julius was cash-rich, he got his way and demolished the single-storey structure. The new house bears no resemblance

to the old, double as it is in size and grandeur, yet it somehow continues to bear the hallmark of that bygone era, perched as it is on the original plot of land on that dreary street in one of the poorest stretches of Seshego.

The township lies about ten kilometres west of Polokwane, according to the traditional measure that covers the distance between one post office and another. It sits at the end of Nelson Mandela Drive that connects it to the city centre and beyond. Many of the houses have been spruced up in the last few years and row after row of neat and well-kept homes now line many of Seshego's streets, yet Masakaneng still remains the poor cousin of the sprawl.

The houses there are run-down and dilapidated, and without fail they all hark back to the 1960s, when the separation of whites from blacks meant not only substandard housing for the latter, but the creation of a monotonous feature on the social landscape of urban South Africa.

The pokey-looking units feature side by side on streets that zigzag through the area. All of the dwellings sit just a few metres back from the street, some behind hedges, high walls or low-lying partial fences, while others sit behind nothing at all and gape out vacantly onto the dusty roads. By and large they vary little and are devoid of character. Pride of ownership in many instances is non-existent and looking at those houses today, it is not difficult to imagine the environment that Julius Malema grew up in.

As a child he shared the back bedroom with his mother, an aunt and some of his cousins. On a quiet night as many as six of them would tuck down to sleep in that confined space.

'I slept with my mother until my cousins started laughing at me,' he remembers. After that he found his place on the floor along with the rest of the young ones.

His grandmother, his grandfather while he still lived there, and some other family members slept in the second bedroom and the floor space of the kitchen was put to good use to cater for the rest.

'It was a good time,' recalls Sarah, who has a hardened but optimistic outlook on life. 'We had nothing, but we shared everything we had with one another. Everything we had belonged to all of us. It wasn't ideal. But that's how it was.'

As she sketches the early days of Julius's life, she paints a picture of a young boy who had an upbringing that was no different from that of thousands of other African youth from that era. He knew nothing but poverty. He was a second-class citizen in his own country. He was reared among his extended family, in his case the majority of whom were women, and he learned to raise his voice at a young age if he wanted to be heard.

He attended local schools and was brought up speaking Sepedi. He was a ruffian, a young hustler who scraped through life and who lived for life on the streets, where he would while away his time from one end of the day to the next.

The Malema home was not a political one, nor was it an ANC house, not because the family didn't have an appetite for the struggle or what it stood for, but because its members were trying to eke out an existence and were mindful of the repressive apartheid legislation that made most forms of black-led political activity a crime. People like the Malemas could ill afford to find themselves on the wrong side of the law.

Nor was it a house of books or lofty teaching. And it wasn't a particularly religious home. The Malemas were simply a very ordinary and very poor family. And though Sarah cut her cloth accordingly, it was often the case that money was so tight that Julius would be forced to find his own way.

He went from street to street collecting old tin cans and bottles and any other items that could possibly be recycled and then he would haggle for the best price. When the going got very tough, he would invariably end up knocking at the doors of neighbours at mealtimes.

Daisy Sebate, then a well-known political activist in the township, remembers how Julius would put his head around her door just as the food was being dished out onto the plates, his impeccable timing an indirect plea for a place at the table.

'But at least he asked, even if he did it in his own way,' Ramaphakela points out. 'He didn't steal. He didn't snatch. That's what most of them did. But he didn't.'

Nor did he beg.

'Never,' Julius says in a tone of fierce pride when I put it to him later. 'I would never allow myself to do that.'

But begging is what most of the youth of Masakaneng resorted to. They would go to Pietersburg and find a street corner to work and when begging didn't yield the returns they wanted, they turned to petty crime. To these young tsotsis, dark habits came naturally and from glue sniffing many of them sank into a larger underworld and went on to become big gangsters.

'But Malema was streetwise,' Sebate remembers. 'He was a survivor and he knew how to get by.'

Julius Malema was thirteen when apartheid came to an end and he lived the rest of his formative years in the democratic dispensation. But for him and many others, 1994 did not bring transformation overnight. His teen years were very tough and the Malema family still struggled to get by. The poverty that hung over that household in some ways became even more endemic because theirs was one of the families that 1994 left behind.

Though Malema is often criticised for trading on his past and citing the fact that his mother was a domestic worker, cleaning

up the mess of people more privileged than herself, it is a fact that he was reared in miserable hardship.

He might have little to complain about today, but the early years of his life, his most important years, were cruel. He was also reared in a city over which the stench of racism still hangs.

Modern-day Polokwane still has a strong Afrikaner feel to it. In 1884 the Zuid-Afrikaansche Republiek bought the eastern half of a large farm called Sterkloop and two years later it was proclaimed the site of a new town called Pietersburg, which was named after Commandant-General Petrus Jacobus Joubert. But during the Second (Great) Boer War that followed in 1899, one of the country's thirty-one concentration camps set up by the British was established in the town: the Pietersburg camp housed more than four thousand Afrikaner women and children. Not surprisingly, the town developed a strong Afrikaner identity in the post-war years. It was also the centre of an agricultural heartland and after apartheid was introduced in 1948, it became a service point for many of the surrounding bantustans.

By the time Julius began to get his head around the ANC and the struggle against apartheid, the Afrikaners were about to face loss for a second time and they began to cling to their Afrikaner identity. A 'them' and 'us' mentality settled into the town, perhaps made even more stark by its size. Pietersburg was not a large urban centre and was only proclaimed a city in 1992, but when it became the seat of the provincial government two years later, it attracted tens of thousands of Africans from all over what was then called the Northern Province. Afrikaners found themselves at the wrong end of the pecking order. They felt threatened and they closed in on themselves. And it was within that social divide that Malema grew up, on one side of the society of Pietersburg.

All told, his early years made him fearless, as well as defiant. It was a period in his life that turned him into an angry hothead.

That anger stayed with him as he established his political whereabouts because it was inevitable that a young man of Malema's character would seek out the mischief that came with the heady days immediately before and after the end of apartheid in 1994.

Chapter 5

Rising through the ranks

Julius Malema in retrospect. That was the tricky part about documenting his early years in politics while he was at his peak in the ANC: his story was relayed so far after the fact that a thick haze of fancy had begun to obscure the early Malema years, particularly in his hometown of Polokwane. Though he was based in Johannesburg around the time that I was charting that early chapter of his life, he was, without any doubt, the most powerful person in the Limpopo capital, if not throughout the province as well. Weeding out the cheerleaders was hellishly difficult.

Then along came Freddie Ramaphakela and he began to piece together that era for me. It is he who lays claim to 'discovering' Malema, a badge he wears with great pride – and with Malema's blessing, it has to be noted. To be sure, his recall of that time had also acquired a favourable construction of its own. But here's how he tells it.

In 1989, just three days before the anniversary of 16 June, the day in 1976 when thousands of students in Soweto raged against the compulsory introduction of Afrikaans as the medium of instruction in schools, Ramaphakela found himself on the wrong side of the white police force. The twenty-four-year-old was a member of Umkhonto we Sizwe (MK), the armed wing of the

ANC, and according to him, he was attached to a cell at the blacks-only University of the North (what is today the University of Limpopo), located about forty kilometres east of Polokwane. In the apartheid era the university was a hotbed of resistance, and though Ramaphakela was not a high-profile target of the security forces, his movements were nonetheless monitored, particularly in his home township of Seshego, or so he claims.

On that day, 13 June, Ramaphakela was holding court on the stoep of the Corner Store, the general grocer in front of the Malema family's house in Masakaneng, with six young boys who were quizzing him about the struggle.

Malema was one of the six and he was eight years old at the time.

Ramaphakela wanted them to understand the basics of the fight against white domination, but he knew he would have to simplify his message. These boys were young, the oldest among them no more than ten or eleven years old. So he gave it to them in basic terms.

Had their mothers ever told them how they suffered at work under their white bosses? Had they ever seen a white person work in a kitchen? How often did they see a mini-bus taxi packed with white people going to and from work? Did they know of any whites who worked for blacks?

'That is how unfair and how wrong the system is,' he told them. 'It is set up to work against us. Whites don't give blacks a chance in our own country. And we are trying to change that.'

'*De boy ga a na verstaan,*' Malema said in local slang. He was suggesting the boys wouldn't be able to grasp what Ramaphakela was saying. It is possible that the eight-year-old didn't understand it either, but his pride wouldn't allow him to admit that.

So Ramaphakela trotted out one or two more examples and while he was in full spiel, a police van pulled up outside the shop and two officers jumped out. With that, the young boys skedaddled. But Malema stayed put.

He backed away towards the wall of the shop, but he didn't run.

Some tough words between Ramaphakela and the officers got out of hand and within seconds he saw the knuckles of one of their fists within a whisker of his right eye. As he tried to duck the blow, the second officer kicked him in the stomach and sent him reeling to the ground.

Ramaphakela wanted to run.

'But then I thought, how could I? I had just been telling these young boys about the importance of fighting the fight. Julius was still standing there. And as I tried to defend myself, I heard Julius shout out, "*Hey wena. O ska betha dai man.*"'

The officers didn't heed the young boy's plea not to hit his older friend, but Ramaphakela remembers thinking afterwards, 'Now there's someone who's fearless and not afraid to fight.'

When in the months that followed Ramaphakela, according to himself, decided to start an underground MK for juniors to train them in guerrilla tactics, Malema was one of a handful of youths he decided to bring under his wing.

'I knew they were young and I wasn't about to tell them to get out onto the streets and fight. No. But we knew we needed a backup in case 1994 never happened and it was obvious to me that we needed to begin to train up young boys, just in case.

'But I had to be careful. If their families knew my plans, they would expose me to the police and that would have been the end of me. People were very afraid then.'

Child fighters were not uncommon in struggles on the African continent or elsewhere and around that time in South Africa, the

MK was rounding up teenagers in many townships and sending them off to Uganda for training. But Ramaphakela was recruiting much younger boys, children who were hardly old enough to spell their own names, and he was taking them underground in their own country. It was an outrageous plan. Ramaphakela was also a very small player in a much larger scheme and he was initiating a move that carried infinite potential for disaster.

'That's why I knew I had to do it right,' he says. 'I would start with paramilitary activities. And then, bit by bit, I would make them feel like they are part of the core of the MK, and then the ANC, and then the bigger picture. We didn't know what was ahead of us at that time. Nobody did. Not even the ANC. We could have been headed for a bloodbath. And if we were, we needed resistance.'

It had all the trimmings of a tall story and when I ran it by a few veterans of the MK, they each looked back at me in bewilderment, adamant that the armed wing did not recruit children at any time during the struggle. There was also uncertainty around Ramaphakela's credentials: no one could vouch for his membership of the armed wing while it was still underground in the pre-1990 period.

'Ask him who his commander was,' one of them suggested. 'And then we will know if this is not just another distortion of our history.'

Ramaphakela claimed his commander was Jacob Rapholo, a well-known MK fighter from that era. But according to Rapholo, Ramaphakela only joined MK after the ban had been lifted on all political parties and their armed wings in 1990.

'Freddie was never part of anything underground or anything secret. Never.'

But Ramaphakela stands by his story. He formed a cell and Malema was one of his recruits. Malema also stands by his version of his early life. That's how it was, or at least that's how they want it to be remembered.

What is also true, Malema says, is that it was Ramaphakela who placed the first gun in his hands and taught him how to pull a trigger, be it for the purposes of the formal military training Ramaphakela says it was, or for some kind of street plan he concocted off his own bat.

What is a fact is that he had known Malema ever since he was a young boy. He knew the Malema family, who, like his own, came from Masakaneng. And as Malema was growing up, he became a familiar face to him in that neck of the township's woods, one of the more wayward children in his midst.

'He lived on the streets and he was caught up in everything he shouldn't have been. He was a loudmouth and he was cheeky,' Ramaphakela remembers.

'But he could always sustain an argument until he won it. And he was a fighter – in a physical sense – and to this day I firmly believe that if I hadn't led him into the ANC, I would have put him into boxing.'

As tough as he was, Malema also had the innocence of a child of his age and he laughs today as he thinks back on his outlook then.

'You know, I thought victory would be so easy. If the problem was the whites being in charge, then all we had to do was put the blacks in charge and the problem would be solved.'

It was simply a matter of raising the right flag. They may have had to put up a fight, but nothing that Malema's young mind could not contemplate. Hence he was a ready soldier when Ramaphakela began to rope the young boys in very, very slowly

in the first few months of 1990. There were only four of them and they were carefully hand-picked, their new master told them. And it would be critical that they keep their activities under tight wraps. It was their secret, and theirs alone. One false move, one whisper to family or friends in Masakaneng, and they would be out.

'I told nobody,' Malema says. 'Nobody.'

During their first few months, Ramaphakela talked to them about the basics of the struggle and the importance of armed resistance and why the ANC was resorting to heavier means. He used to take them down to a dry riverbed in a stretch of wasteland at the back of the township and teach them what he felt they needed to know.

He got them to stockpile tyres, from old cars and trucks, down on the riverbed so that they could be used for barricading roads. He talked to them about combat activities. He gave them some physical training. And he eventually taught them how to use a Makarov 9 mm pistol. First he taught them how to focus their aim and then one day, about a year or so later, he loaded it with live ammunition and got each of them to pull the trigger.

'And he taught us how to dismantle it and clean it and put it back together,' Malema remembers.

'I was teaching them to be brave,' Ramaphakela says. 'And even if they were never going to be used in combat activities, I knew I would use their fearlessness to penetrate and gather information and infiltrate other organisations in the township. At some point we wanted to make sure AZAPO [Azanian People's Organisation] never existed in our township. But we didn't want confrontation with them. We wanted to outmanoeuvre them on political strategy. And that's where I knew I could count on the likes of Malema to help with gathering information.'

Malema was only pint-sized at the time, but he was loving it all. His world was changing. Everything around him was taking on a different hue. The mood had shifted. There wasn't the same fear any more. The troubled 1980s had come to an end and shortly after 1990 was ushered in, Nelson Mandela was released from prison. Though Malema had heard mention of the famous prisoner, it was only when Madiba walked free that Malema began to understand his importance.

The ANC was unbanned around the same time and with it the veil of secrecy was lifted from politics and there was talk of little else on the streets of Seshego. Beyond the northern township, South Africa was dizzy with expectation and Julius Malema found himself caught up in the thick of it all.

'But I don't remember Malema being with us in 1990,' says Thabo Makunyane, who had been released from Robben Island a year earlier. When the party was unbanned the following February, Makunyane was appointed its provincial convenor until such time as the members organised themselves into formal structures. Hence he was familiar with all of the cadres, old and new. But Malema wasn't one of them.

'Definitely not,' says Makunyane. 'But then again, I spent a lot of time travelling throughout the province.'

But Malema talks about how shortly after he celebrated his ninth birthday he was drafted into the Masupatsela, the children's social wing of the ANC, and donned his marshal's uniform for the first time. Pietersburg was organising a homecoming rally for Elias Motsoaledi, a local man (and uncle of the national health minister Aaron Motsoaledi) who had been released along with the Rivonia Trialists a few months earlier. A ceremony was planned at the University of the North that would be followed by a mass rally in the stadium in Seshego, within walking distance of Malema's house.

By then the young boy had also captured the attention of Lawrence Mapoulo, the erstwhile executive mayor of the Capricorn district of Limpopo. Back then he was a taxi driver who conveniently joined the Seshego branch of the ANC shortly after the liberation movement was unbanned in 1990. The branch operated out of a small unit over a shop at the Mabenkeleng shopping complex in Zone 1 and Malema made sure that he made himself known to Mapoulo. The youngster was like his shadow, constantly nipping at his heels. Everywhere he turned, every event he organised, every catfight that took place, the young boy was there.

Mapoulo was one of many who helped organise Motsoaledi's homecoming. They were expecting a record turnout at the Seshego stadium and he needed all the help he could get so he roped Malema in as one of the marshals. He told him he was to be there at the crack of dawn and he was to be decked out in full regalia.

Malema wore his old school clothes: a short-sleeved khaki shirt and matching full-length khaki trousers. Pinned to the epaulettes was an ANC badge and pulled down over his unkempt Afro hairstyle was a black beret, the signature cap of resistance.

It didn't matter to him that the clothes were hand-me-downs. He didn't think twice about the fact that the soles of his shoes had already worn thin. The ANC had called him to duty. In his young mind, he was a comrade now; a big man in the making.

'And there's nothing that you can tell me about the ANC that I don't already know,' he would often say during his heyday as a member of the ruling party.

Nobody in his family – not his grandmother, his mother, his aunts or his cousins – was aware of what the junior member of the family was up to. It was surely just innocent mischief, they thought, the stuff of young boys.

According to his grandmother, it was not until 1993, when he was twelve and hopped onto a bus and travelled to Johannesburg to attend Chris Hani's funeral, that they realised he was kicking up dust on the fringes of the struggle, a fact she likes to share with a certain degree of pride.

Throughout that April day when Hani was laid to rest on the outskirts of Johannesburg, Malema was nowhere to be found in Seshego. Not even his friends knew of his plans to sneak onto one of the buses that was taking the comrades to Gauteng.

'Every time I tried to get rid of them, I would turn a corner and they would be there,' he remembers. When he finally managed to shake them off, he found his moment and darted for the nearest bus.

He would later tell the Johannesburg High Court during the hate speech trial in 2011 that he was carrying a pistol when he got on that bus, which he claimed the leadership of the ANC had given him.

Makunyane was coordinating the buses that day and he doesn't remember Malema being armed, though Ramaphakela insists he gave the pistol to him.

'It was a Makarov. It belonged to the MK. I was using it and I gave it to him,' he says.

For the second if not the third or fourth time during our conversation, Makunyane raises his eyes in mock surprise.

Whether or not Julius was armed was the farthest thing from Sarah's mind, however. She just didn't know where he was that day.

'We knew nothing about what he was up to until he came home,' she says.

This was not something she or the other family members took in their stride. Though the ANC was by then unbanned, fear of

politics was still widespread. But they could do nothing to stop the young boy at that point. Every spare moment he had, he gave to his new-found comrades.

'By then we all knew him,' says Makunyane. 'He was everywhere. And he was a popular youth.'

In the run-up to the first democratic elections of 1994, Malema did whatever odd job was asked of him. He hung posters. He helped with registrations. He did the footwork in organising events.

'Not long after that, I even bought him his first cellphone,' Makunyane remembers. He was a ready foot soldier for the cause and the comrades helped him as much as he helped them.

'He would come looking for taxi money,' recalls Sam Rampedi, who worked in the provincial structures of the party and later in provincial government. 'And I would give it to him. He was just a young activist and his heart and mind was in his work. He was the kind of youth you wouldn't hesitate to help. He was determined. And it was all in the name of the ANC.'

Though Malema insists the early 1990s marked his first steps in politics, it is unlikely that he had any substantial grasp of formal politics at that time. Probably he was lured more by the mischief and excitement of that period than by any real understanding of what South Africa was about to witness or the complexities that had brought the country to this point.

It is also possible that his upbringing, fragmented and difficult as it was, played an even bigger part in his decision to throw himself wholeheartedly into the bosom of the ANC. Malema never knew what it was to be shouldered by an older male figure. As I have mentioned in earlier pages, he had never known his father. His grandfather had left the house before he was born. The only older male in his life was his uncle who lived with him, but who had suffered a nervous breakdown.

Then at the age of eight or nine Malema found himself among people who were old enough to be his parents: men and women who regaled him with great stories about the struggle and exciting yarns about exile or what life was like behind bars for those who had chosen to stay behind, and the efforts it took overall to put an end to white rule.

'There was only one person that I was older than and that was [Jacob] Lebogo. But the rest of them, each of these people could have been my father,' he says. And they each had an enormous influence over his young mind.

Malema was deep in his element, as any child of his age would have been. In his mind, these people were heroes. He was in awe of them and he could hardly believe his luck. From a fairly hellish life and a humdrum township upbringing, Julius Malema woke up one morning to find himself in the thick of a liberation movement that was no longer outlawed, a political party that was the talk of the country and which was steadily marching towards victory in South Africa's first democratic elections of 1994. It couldn't get much better than this in the young boy's mind. And there was no going back. From then on, he began to live and breathe the liberation movement in whose structures he was becoming embedded, starting out in the youth and student movements that were then being established in schools all over the country.

Malema had attended schools in the township, starting out at Mponegele Lower Primary before moving to Kgobokanang Senior Primary, a school he left because of the corporal punishment being dispensed. He then spent a few years at Letlotlo Senior Primary nearby before attending Mohlakaneng High School, which was also in the township.

It was during his years at Letlotlo and Mohlakaneng, in the years immediately after 1994, that Malema began to cut his teeth as a political activist. He had joined the Congress of South African Students (COSAS) while he was still in primary school. As soon as he turned fourteen he joined the ANCYL, which had been formally re-established in 1991. He kept his ties with older comrades in the ANC all the while, attending rallies and meetings whenever he could, growing more and more confident about himself and his new place in the world as he shed his schoolboy carapace.

It was a time of great change in South Africa, and it was no different for school students. They were speaking out about their rights, demanding improved learning conditions and politicising playgrounds with the establishment of student representative councils (SRCs).

For the black teachers, who had spent their entire professional lives compromised in the system of Bantu Education, serving under the white-led regime, what they were witnessing worried them. They were feeling a new kind of unease and this latest threat was coming from their own students, who were rocking their authority. The new black-led government was promising to bring change, but they were not sure what kind of change and what that would mean for them. Their initial reaction was to resist it.

Jeff Legodi was the principal of Mohlakaneng when Malema was a student there and he tried to prevent the students from establishing an SRC. Malema claims he was expelled because of it, though Legodi and other teachers say Malema was never forced to leave the school.

Malema also takes credit for leading a campaign to dislodge Legodi, who was part of the management structures of the old

set-up and regarded as a stumbling block to reform by the new authorities. But Legodi insists he resigned of his own accord in 1999.

'I had more influence over Malema than he could ever have had over me,' he claims all these years later.

While the former principal is set on downplaying Malema's role as the school ringleader, there are a few truths that point to the raffish and fearless nature of the budding politician.

Onismas Letlalo was a teacher of history and he was fond of laying down his own rules and whipping his students into line. But one day he went too far and gave some young girls a severe hiding that sent them limping to Malema for help. He called Joyce Mashamba, who was then the Limpopo MEC for Education, and told her what was happening. Within minutes, she and her team were marching through the school gates demanding to know what had happened.

Journalists who reported on that era and who covered the student protests remember Malema well and how he would inevitably creep into their stories. A ringleader, as he is now, he was usually a part of the township student protests, if not the one who started them, and was always on the front line with something to say.

'Malema would never allow anyone else to speak in his name or in the name of the students,' recalls Thomas Namathe, another senior teacher at the school. 'If the media came to cover a story and we, as the staff, tried to give our point of view, he would be the first to speak up on the side of the learners.'

Legodi suggests this should come as no surprise because Malema's school fees were paid by ANC members and the youth was a willing handler of their dirty work in return. Although the former principal refuses to say exactly who paid the youth's

fees, if there's truth in it at all, it still did not stop Malema from speaking out against his own party. In 1997 he was elected provincial chairperson of COSAS in Limpopo, a position that allowed him to cast his net further afield than the township of Seshego.

'He had his mind set on that position for a long time,' says Makunyane. 'And he wouldn't stop until he got it.'

'I was enjoying student politics,' Malema says as he thinks back to that era. 'It was clear to me what our rights were as students and what we should fight for. It was well defined. I could see the path of student politics clearly.'

But not long after he became the provincial chairperson, Malema began to show another side to his character. Coupled with his ambition and militancy was blatant arrogance. In 1998, he decided to take on Joe Phaahla, who had replaced Mashamba as the MEC for Education (and who is currently serving in Zuma's government). Malema felt Phaahla was dragging his heels when it came to reform.

You are a 'contraception to transformation', Malema told him in a public statement he circulated widely and on every media platform that would care to entertain it. The ANC tried to rein in Malema. As if the gaffe in his choice of words was not in itself bad enough, it was not right to turn on one of his own in this way, they tried to tell him.

'Phaahla asked me to have a word with him,' Makunyane remembers. 'But, hey … ,' he says, shaking his head slowly from side to side. Malema was beyond talking to.

Phaahla threatened to sue Malema if he didn't lay the matter to rest. But his words also fell on deaf ears. Malema had little or no fear.

Those in the ANC and on other political platforms who express surprise at Malema's rise ought to think back to his teen

years and the kind of person he was. His political character has been a long time in the making but was never fully captured.

As much as Malema lacked fear he also lacked focus at school. He was distracted by his political activism and his schoolwork hardly got a look in. His teachers say they couldn't get through to him, that his mind was elsewhere. That did not make him the school dunce, however. He was a good listener, when he cared to listen. And he had a remarkable ability for recall. They just couldn't get him to settle down to books.

Nor did he give a hoot about his appearance and he would file into the classroom most mornings looking the worse for wear. He was scrawny and skinny and at the time wore a large Afro. Yet despite his waif-like frame he struggled to get a school uniform to fit him, so he invariably wore his long school pants flying at half-mast throughout his high school years.

The ill-fitting trousers were not exclusive to Malema. In township South Africa they were called 'Don't touch my shoes' and his peers remember that he wore them each school day of every week. Outside school hours his wardrobe varied little. He was a carefree youth who wore open sandals and short pants, always topped with an ANC T-shirt.

Not today. When he was in his late twenties, Malema began to wear top-end designer labels and all sorts of gimmickry associated with his new money and his puffed-up image of himself. But as a teenager, he had no interest whatsoever in fashion and that he didn't look too sleek bothered him little at the time. He found his kudos in activism instead.

In June 2000 he decided to run for national president of COSAS, a position that was ironically held at the time by Lebogang Maile, the man who challenged him for the position of ANCYL president in 2011. As a provincial chairperson of

COSAS, Malema sat on the NEC of the student body and he enjoyed the support of many of his peers in that group in his bid for the presidency, Maile included.

'It wasn't difficult to support him because he was very courageous. He was militant, when we needed militancy. And he was a leader. That much went without saying,' says Maile today of the Malema of yesterday.

However, at the branch level it was a different matter. The vast majority of branches favoured Kenny Morolong, who was the provincial chairperson of COSAS in North West province. A month ahead of the June conference, when all the branches had spoken and nominated their preferred candidate, it was clear that Morolong would win the race. He had the backing of six provinces, while Malema had only Limpopo, Gauteng and Northern Cape behind him.

'But just a few days before the conference, rape charges mysteriously surfaced out of nowhere,' Morolong remembers. 'I was accused of raping Mosa Molale,' a woman Morolong was dating at the time.

'There were no criminal charges preferred against me. There was no criminal investigation to determine whether such allegations existed. I was simply told that I had raped a member of COSAS, a woman who was a member of the provincial executive committee in my province. And the NEC suspended me,' on the grounds that it couldn't field a candidate with such serious allegations against his name.

Morolong was innocent; he hadn't raped Molale or any other woman, but he knew he was a threat to Malema's ambitions so he decided to defy the suspension and attend the conference, which took place at 17 Shaft in Johannesburg. But security denied him entry and when he was turned away, the delegates, whose support he still enjoyed, began to rally behind him.

Fikile Mbalula, who was then the secretary-general of the ANCYL, was also attending the COSAS conference. As a senior to the COSAS delegates, he appealed to them to negotiate their way out of the crisis and try to settle on a consensus leadership. He proposed that Morolong would be president and Malema would be his deputy, but the delegates refused to accept it. They wanted to elect their president and deputy president by a vote only and refused to entertain any other route. The tensions mounted and descended into an ugly brawl.

'I started receiving death threats. I was told I wouldn't live. I even remember having to go to the bathroom with two well-built men escorting me,' says Morolong.

The havoc continued and the violence worsened.

'I remember one poster being pushed into my face that read "We can't vote for a rapist". I will never forget that.'

Eventually Molale spoke up and denied that she had been raped or that she had laid charges, but her words came too late. Some senior ANC people were brought in to try to break the deadlock, but to no avail. Winnie Madikizela-Mandela was then called in and briefed about what was going on. She quickly assessed the matter for herself and a short while later she disbanded the conference. It resumed a year later, but Morolong was no longer a contender.

'Every time I tried to attend a COSAS meeting after that, I was threatened or bullied. And I eventually resigned. It was one of the most painful periods of my life. Even though it was only student politics, and it might not sound like much to you, it meant everything to me. Coming from my background, I knew what it meant to fight for our rights. And back then, I really thought this would be my life. But I just couldn't take it any more. And I left.'

A short while later Morolong started to drink heavily and his weakness for alcohol eventually got the better of him, reaching an all-time low at the end of 2002 when Popo Molefe, who was then the premier of North West province, had him checked into rehab. He celebrated his twenty-first birthday in the clinic and was discharged only in May 2003.

'And I have never drunk alcohol since, though I will always be a recovering alcoholic,' he says all these years later.

Today he's a senior member of the ANC in North West, but youth politics passed him by entirely. Malema, meanwhile, had pushed on to greater heights. A year later he ran again for the position of president of COSAS.

But in the run-up to that conference he found himself in a bind. He had a physical temper to match his vicious tongue and he pummelled a peer's face so badly with his fists that his opponent's mother wouldn't allow him to leave the house for weeks because his face was such a mess. She threatened to bring charges against Malema.

The COSAS elections were only a few months away and Malema knew that if the boy laid a charge, there was a good chance he wouldn't make it. So he asked Ramaphakela to talk to the boy's family instead. Ramaphakela obliged and claims it turned out to be nothing that a small 'donation' couldn't put right. When I reminded Malema of this all these years later, he threw his head back and laughed.

Malema won the election comfortably. That was in 2001 and he was twenty, though he was still in high school, which would not have been at all uncommon at that time, or even now. He moved to Johannesburg to be close to the national offices of the student movement, which were housed in the ANC's then headquarters at Shell House in Noord Street, close to the taxi rank.

Malema headed straight for the vibrant inner-city suburb of Hillbrow with his friends Victor Chepape and Priscilla Monama and they rented a small pad in the Fontana block of flats. A brief stint in the notorious high-rise Ponte Towers followed until he finally settled down in a flat opposite Oriental Plaza in Fordsburg, on the edge of the city centre.

By then the school books were well and truly forgotten, despite the fact that Malema was still enrolled at Mohlakaneng and registered to sit his Matric examinations at the end of 2001. But Seshego was four or more hours away from Johannesburg by car and given the physical distance that separated him from his classroom, Malema decided instead to attend a few classes at Prudence High School in Tladi, Soweto. Mostly, though, he stayed away from school altogether.

Malema still sat his Matric at the end of that year, but fared badly and failed most of his subjects. He got a C in English, a D in History and an E in his mother tongue, Sepedi, as well as in Afrikaans. There was an F in Geography and a G in Woodwork, both of them at standard grade.

Years later, his Matric results started popping up in email in-boxes all over the country when one of his many adversaries tried to shame him. Maropeng, the mother of his child, contacted him to warn him what was happening, but there was little he could do about it. Before long a copy of his results certificate landed in the lap of the media, who were quick to splash it across the front pages of the country's main newspapers. It was the G in Woodwork that tickled most minds.

'At least we know he'll never make a cabinet maker,' quipped one wit at the time, evidently without the benefit of foresight.

In his own defence, Malema says he never actually wrote the Woodwork exam. Rather than not show up, 'I just went in and

wrote my name at the top of the exam and walked out' without writing another word, he says.

Did he feel shame or embarrassment about his results?

'That's what it was,' he says. 'I was an activist first. I still am. I always will be.'

Despite what he says, I believe the exposure of his school results bruised Malema in a big way. By nature, he's a very proud person. He is also extremely clever, despite the public opinion of him as a young buffoon, but he had failed that one exam against which so many South Africans benchmark an individual's intellectual ability. That was the key point about Malema, which has always been overlooked: he didn't have a formal education or training worth speaking of but that does not make him stupid. His ability to manipulate information – one of the key defining features of intelligence – is as acute as his ability to recall it, which is what makes him the cunning and wily character that he is.

His other big failing in the eyes of the public was his poor grasp of English, which is not his first language but his fourth (Sepedi, Sesotho and Afrikaans are his others). When he began to introduce himself, his iron nerve and his revolutionary posture to South Africa in those early months of 2008, he spoke a vulgar kind of English that was made all the more crass by the content of his political messages. It was no surprise therefore that the chattering classes had such a bellyful of laughs when his desultory Matric results started doing the rounds.

Malema did not make much of it publicly at the time, but what was telling was a short text message he forwarded to me a few months later. He had received it from the University of South Africa (UNISA), where he was studying for a two-year diploma in Youth Development. In a few words it explained that

he had completed his two-year diploma in Youth Development. By forwarding it to me, it somehow seemed important to him to have it known. One small detail weighted with sentiment.

A few weeks later he enrolled for a Bachelor of Arts degree at UNISA, which he feels will enhance his political career.

Again, it is not something he tends to talk about much in public, but even in 2013 as the EFF was being launched and when he was facing another court hearing over his corruption charges, he juggled his time to ensure his studies did not suffer. He did the same in 2011 during the local government elections. Once he had cast his vote, he went home to study for an exam that was scheduled for the following day. That was the day the counting of the votes was under way and Malema was nowhere to be seen at the Pretoria count centre. He didn't show his face again until the end of the week, but when he did, he was up to his usual tricks, telling reporters he was unwilling to debate Lindiwe Mazibuko, then the national spokesperson of the Democratic Alliance (DA).

She was only the 'tea gal', he argued. And she should stay in the kitchen serving 'the madam'. It was the madam he wanted to meet. The madam was, of course, Helen Zille.

'The madam' was, and regrettably still is, the title the 'black maids' use for their white bosses, at the request of the white women. (Equally unfortunate is the title of 'the master' that is reserved for the white men of many households.) For millions of South Africans, there could have been no title more apt for Zille than 'the madam'.

Zille, whom Malema on other occasions referred to as a 'political toddler', has regularly been the butt of his debased sense of humour. A few years ago she had Botox treatment on her face and openly admitted to it, because many believed her stern look was undermining her political profile. Malema was

quick to pounce, accusing her of 'using Michael Jackson tactics'. He later warned the public that 'she is plastic' and 'If you can fake your own face, what about the policies?', a comment that got the whole country laughing.

The bite of his wit has always been legendary. In the run-up to the 2009 general elections the running commentary was questioning the ANC's ability to secure a two-thirds majority under Zuma's leadership, to which Malema casually responded, 'We are tired of a two-thirds majority. Our aim is a three-thirds majority.' He talked about how the Youth League was like a factory that churned out great leaders like the late Nelson Mandela, but how Mangosuthu Buthelezi, the leader of the black opposition Inkatha Freedom Party, was nothing but a 'factory fault'. (To the surprise of many, Malema later apologised to Buthelezi in the run-up to the 2014 elections, by which time the EFF was contesting its first national elections and needed more partners than enemies if the party was to see its way through.)

Wit to one side, though, there has always been a threatening and dangerous side to Malema. In 2002, he kicked up a political storm in the centre of the city when he led COSAS in a violent march throughout the downtown area of Johannesburg.

The Department of Education had said it wanted to enforce a ruling that the gates to all schools be locked during teaching hours to try to keep crime from their doors as a safety measure for its learners.

COSAS was against the move and decided to stage a protest in response. The authorities forbade the march, but the thousands-strong student movement defied the order and went on a rampage. The marchers looted shops, smashed windows, turned hawkers' stands upside down, damaged parked cars and left an unsightly trail of destruction in their wake.

Malema was the ringleader and the leadership of the ANC called him aside a few days later, demanding that he do something about what had happened. Malema shrugged off this request.

In the meantime, he had been drawn under the wing of Madikizela-Mandela, who began to groom him in the art of politics and rebellion. He spent hours in her company, and often days at her Soweto home, where he found shelter through thick and thin and he was quick to return the compliment when she, as a member of parliament, was convicted of fraud and theft in 2003. He told the courts they were being racist towards the Mother of the Nation, as she is widely known.

'We are prepared to do anything in our power to ensure that she is not in jail,' he touted at the time. 'If that means burning the prison she is locked in, so be it.'

She didn't forget him for it and sat by his side throughout the nine-day hate speech trial in 2011.

'He is my product,' she later claimed.

'She taught me public speaking and confidence,' he said in response.

'His rebellious attitude is part of the process of growing up,' she added. 'He will make a great leader one day.'

She was not to know then that he would one day end up leading his own party in opposition to the ANC. Malema has courted Madikizela-Mandela heavily to join him in the EFF, sending Dali Mpofu as the messenger, but she has declined, though she has continued to praise him and insists he will become a significant threat to the ANC, if not now then in the not-too-distant future.

When his tenure as COSAS president ended in 2003, Malema returned to Polokwane. His home friends had been lobbying for

him to come back and run for the position of provincial secretary of the ANCYL.

'We wanted a more militant Youth League to bring about change in Limpopo because we had entered into a slump,' says Lehlogonolo Masoga. He had been a close friend of Malema's since the mid-1990s when their paths first crossed, at a time when Masoga was rising through the provincial ranks of the South African Students Congress (SASCO) while Malema was working his way up through the provincial structures of COSAS. Though the two young men were different in character, they both opted for a militant style of politics.

'I liked his bravery,' Masoga says. 'And I liked his fearlessness. He stands by what he believes in. And he is never afraid to put words on his views. Not everyone has the kind of courage that he has. And very few can think on their feet like he does. And he had what we were looking for in a provincial secretary back then. We were looking for change and we knew we would have to put up a fight.'

'You see, at that time the Youth League had become a transmitter belt for the ANC,' says David Masondo, who was a member of the ANCYL as well as the Young Communist League then. Today he is one of the disgraced members of the Limpopo cabinet that was led by Cassel Mathale.

'We were concerned about the macroeconomic policies that were being introduced by Thabo Mbeki, but they were not really being contested by the Youth League. So we had to shake it up,' says Masondo.

Julius Malema was nominated to do the shaking. He challenged Harris Rikhotso for the position of provincial secretary at the end of 2003 and he won the contest with ease. Masondo was elected provincial chairman at the same time.

It was a position Malema held for several terms and with each passing year his power base began to grow. He did not confine himself to the ranks of the youth, but began to mingle closely with the provincial leaders of the ANC and through them was exposed to the possibilities that came with party politics.

Chapter 6

Malema becomes a man

As fast as Julius Malema's political life was changing, so too were his personal circumstances, and 2006 marked one of the best and worst years of his life: he fell in love, fathered a child, lost his mother and, at the heel of it all, found his footing in the ANC.

While he was living in Johannesburg he had dated a young woman named Trudy, and though he was a wild, young thing enjoying city life, she remained his steady girlfriend until he returned to Polokwane and met Maropeng Ramohlale, in whom he met his match.

'Maropeng is from Seshego,' Malema once told me. 'She's a township girl and she has a township mentality.' She was well able to fight her corner is what he was saying. She also gave him a run for his money and for that he loved her.

I remember once, long after they broke up, sitting with him in his Johannesburg home chatting about something or other that was entirely unrelated to his personal life, and while we were talking he reached for his laptop and brought up a photograph of her that she had sent to him a few days earlier, dolled up in all her finery to attend a friend's wedding.

'This is her,' he said as he handed his laptop to me. 'This is Maropeng.' They had been apart for four or more years at that

time, but there was no doubt about the soft spot he still had for her. He would later concede that breaking up with her was one of his biggest personal regrets.

In the early days of their relationship she would often accompany him to rallies or other ANC gatherings, though the interest in politics was all his. One evening, early in 2006, they had arranged to go to a rally together, but when he arrived at her parents' Seshego home she told him she needed to talk.

His response was curt. 'Later, later,' he said, as he manoeuvred the car out onto the street. 'We need to talk,' she said again.

'Sure,' he told her, 'but later.' He was pressed for time.

'I'm pregnant,' she told him.

He felt as if every drop of blood began to drain from him in that moment. He needed something to hold on to and he pressed his palms into the steering wheel, but his hands were already wet with the beads of sweat that were pumping from his palms and he couldn't keep his grip. He was in a state of shock.

'That night I got so drunk,' he says. 'Yo, I didn't know what to do, or who to tell. I never thought it would happen like that.'

The first person Julius turned to was Cassel Mathale, a man twenty years his senior and who was then the provincial secretary of the ANC. Despite the age gap, he and Julius had become good friends after Malema's return to Polokwane, and as one of his main confidants, it was to him Malema turned the following day.

It was no big deal, Cassel told him. He was to stand by Maropeng. She would have the child. Everything would turn out okay.

He then told his grandmother and the old woman gave him similar words of advice.

As the weeks passed Julius began to settle into the idea of becoming a father. Then one evening, a few months later, as the

couple were sitting together on the sofa in his house, Maropeng put his hand on her belly as the baby began to kick.

'Hey, what's the problem?' he asked her, in that distinctively gruff manner of his, instinct telling him to pull his hand away. But the two feet kicking inside Maropeng touched him in every respect, 'and then I started to demand to touch,' he remembers. 'And I thought something was wrong if I was no longer called to touch, or if he didn't kick.'

When Maropeng was about seven months pregnant, Florah, Julius's mother, died. It was a sudden death and it tore him apart. He had sailed through life without any real check on his emotions and his mother's death left him reeling.

Hence when Maropeng began what turned out to be a drawn-out labour a couple of months later, Julius feared the worst. He brought her to the hospital and remembers seeing her writhing in pain and gasping for breath, struggling to bring the baby into the world. He feared the worst.

'I thought she was going to die. I thought: "No, man. Not again. Not two deaths: her and the baby, just after my mother."'

He sped home to relay to his grandmother what was happening at the hospital and she quickly put his mind at ease.

'She's not ill,' the old woman assured him. 'She's not going to die. She's giving birth. That's natural.'

A few hours later Maropeng gave birth to a baby boy and the couple named him Ratanang, the Sepedi for 'love each other', Julius says.

It was 14 October, exactly two months after his mother's death.

The couple weren't married but that didn't stop them settling into family life. Julius adored his son, his only child, and enjoyed every minute he had with him in those early days.

But the bigger family, the ANC, was also beginning to call on him. The landmark Polokwane conference was only a year away and the party had a battle on its hands to unseat Thabo Mbeki.

Malema was being called to task. He began to spend more and more time away from home, attending rallies, visiting branches, plotting the Polokwane putsch, and it wasn't long before his political life took a toll on his relationship with Maropeng and the pair eventually went their separate ways.

Though she is now married and settled in Mpumalanga, Ratanang continues to feature prominently in Malema's life. He co-rears him as best he can and he has never left any doubt in my mind about the big place the child occupies in his hectic life. It is always when he speaks about Ratanang that he reveals that softer side of his character, when there is not a trace of aggression or bitterness in his voice.

As Malema's profile began to grow within the ANC, he developed a sense of self-importance that far outweighed his station in life and an arrogance that cost many people their own standing within the party. Though he was a sharp political operator, he was also a conceited bully.

Some branches, and even entire regions, across the province of Limpopo that began to question his leadership style disbanded, only to be relaunched at a later date in accordance with the way Malema wanted them structured, complete with his chosen comrades in the positions that mattered most.

By then, Fikile Mbalula was president of the ANCYL and had become one of the faces of the anti-Mbeki lobby. ANC members had become concerned about the state of democracy within the party, and when they began to question what was regarded as an overly centralised and ossified leadership put in place by Mbeki,

it was Mbalula who emerged as one of the leading voices of that discontent.

Mbalula has a fiery character and is a no less able politician than Malema. He is also an excellent speaker and despite some of his potentially questionable political dealings, he oozes gravitas and charisma and was regarded then as one of the ANC's rising young stars. Over the past few years his standing has waned, though he is still hugely popular among the party membership, even if he appears to have lost his footing somewhat.

Initially Mbalula and Malema didn't see eye to eye. During the early days of the former's presidency of the ANCYL, Malema questioned his hard-line approach to the Congress of South African Trade Unions (COSATU) and the South African Communist Party (SACP). Malema was more left-leaning and he and his provincial peers would be quick to call Mbalula to order when he put pressure on the alliance partners or if he wasn't harsh enough on Mbeki's macroeconomic policy they were rallying against.

'There was a time when Mbalula wanted to disband us,' Malema remembers.

But Malema and Mbalula found common ground on Zimbabwe, when the latter expressed his staunch support for the Zimbabwe African National Union-Patriotic Front (ZANU-PF). They became particularly close politically when in 2006 they began to lobby for Zuma's comeback in the run-up to the Polokwane conference.

Malema was only twenty-five at the time and he was about to become a prominent member of the posse that would cut short Mbeki's career in what would turn out to be a tough and dirty leadership battle. It was fought long and hard for more than two years and wedged a nasty and lasting cleavage in the decades-old

liberation movement, with all who supported Mbeki entrenched on the one side and all who opposed him (rather than necessarily supported Zuma) on the other. Neither faction was going to budge an inch and there would be no compromise.

Thabo Mbeki had been groomed for leadership from an early age and appeared reluctant to step down any time soon, even if he had served his fair share of years at the top. But more than a steadfast grip on power was the belief on his part that this was a motley crew who were about to step into his shoes and begin to pull at the strings of the transition he had been orchestrating for so long.

In the run-up to the Polokwane conference, Mbeki watched a worrying tide rise up and gush towards him, comprising old enemies, some corporate chiefs, the trade union movement and factions from the left whose hopes of a mass insurrection against apartheid he had crushed towards the end of the struggle era in the 1980s.

All these years later, they were about to crush Mbeki, and riding on their shoulders was Zuma, the erstwhile deputy president of the party and the country whom Mbeki had sacked in 2005.

Zuma had been dropped because the corruption charges that were stacked against him were beginning to weigh heavily on the Mbeki presidency. They were linked to the multimillion-rand arms deal scandal from the late 1990s, a hugely fraudulent and controversial contract the financial details of which the ANC has, to this day, managed to keep buried, despite numerous investigations into it in South Africa, Germany, Sweden, England and elsewhere.

Zuma became embroiled in it all when his financial adviser, Schabir Shaik, was found guilty of corruption and fraud in one of

the arms deal contracts. Most certainly Zuma was not alone but Mbeki decided to fire him, fearful that if he did not act decisively and remove him from cabinet, the scrutiny would shift to the government and the glare would go all the way to the top.

Mbeki was foolish if he did not expect a reprisal in some form, but it is unlikely that he would have foreseen Zuma demanding his pound of flesh in so spectacular a fashion as he did in 2007 when he challenged Mbeki for the party leadership, and that it would be Malema, a born foot soldier, who would appear at his side, ready and willing for action.

It was a tough battle, and though Zuma won the leadership in that Polokwane conference it was with only 60 per cent of the votes; slightly less than half of the ANC's voting members were either still with Mbeki or solidly against Zuma in one of the most spectacular fallouts of the arms deal.

There was still a second hurdle to climb, though. The charges against Zuma were still hanging over him and they would have to be removed somehow if he was to have a good run at the 2009 general elections and secure the ANC the comfortable majority it needed to rule in the heavy-handed manner it appeared to desire. If Zuma were to fall at that last hurdle, the chances were that all the colourful characters who had propelled him back to power would do so too. There was no option but to pull out all the stops, at every level, to ensure that their man would walk free.

This second round of battle would not be for the faint-hearted. It called for manoeuvres of an unorthodox nature. Only the fearless could pull this one off. Malema was about to prove himself an ideal candidate for the job.

In the meantime, Mbalula's term as ANCYL president was drawing to a close and he had decided on Malema as his

successor. Mbalula was ambitious and as the curtain came down on the Polokwane conference he was already casting his mind ahead to the party's next elections, in Mangaung in 2012, when he hoped to secure the powerful position of party secretary-general. He would need to ensure the support of the ANCYL, one of the key lobbying blocks, and by having Malema at the helm his future would be secure.

The Youth League's elective conference was scheduled for April 2008, in Mangaung. Yet despite Malema's rise to prominence at Zuma's side in the comeback fight, he didn't have majority support among the youth delegates at that time and he went into that conference with only a couple of provinces behind him. 'But if I didn't have provincial leadership structures behind me, I had a lot of delegates with me,' he recalls.

It was a feature of Malema's appeal: if he didn't have support at the top, he had it on the ground, where it matters most.

Saki Mofokeng was the preferred candidate and he had the majority of provinces behind him. However, Malema was Mbalula's preferred choice and he won the contest by a very narrow margin of 1 883 votes to the 1 696 of his main challenger. The vote was disputed and the conference was subsequently adjourned until June.

By the time June came round Mofokeng surprised many by accepting defeat and calling on all candidates to support Malema and his fellow leadership in the name of party unity. Mofokeng then quickly carved out a niche in business.

Some delegates who supported Malema at the Mangaung conference suggest the vote was rigged. While Malema had the support of many branches, the numbers simply did not add up.

One version of what happened in Mangaung was explained to me in the following way, ironically by a man who was a pro-

Malema delegate. 'We knew the numbers were tight, so we caucused all of the Malema supporters outside the conference hall. And we did a headcount. And with that, we knew how many supporters he had, give or take.

'And as we were caucusing outside, all of the other delegates were inside the hall. They were told to go and register, but then we, the Malema camp, stood in line to vote. So by the time all the other delegates joined the queue, the top of the line was full of Malema people.

'Based on the count we had taken outside the conference centre, we knew what we were dealing with in numbers. So when roughly that same number of people cast their vote, we knew that we would have to "manage" the rest of the delegates that followed, who weren't Malema supporters, if we were to ensure a Malema win. So at a certain point, we stopped the voting,' he told me. And that's how they came up with a narrow margin that favoured Malema.

I have heard other versions of what happened. I have also been told that a group of youth approached ANC Secretary-General Gwede Mantashe with evidence of a twist in the vote but that he refused to entertain their claims. Mantashe denied this when I put it to him.

Lehlogonolo Masoga, Malema's chief campaigner that year, scoffs at any suggestion of a vote rig. Though the pair has had a bitter falling-out since then (a common feature of Malema's personal and political relationships), Masoga had travelled the length and breadth of the country drumming up support for his friend in 2008, because a leg-up for Malema would have served Masoga well.

'I had always stood by him, ever since we became friends. And I was prepared to do so then more than ever.'

While Malema knew that his friend was loyal to him, he was also aware that Masoga had become hugely popular among the delegates he lobbied – and it bothered him. There was only one place at the top and that was his, and for the first time he saw a potential competitor in his old friend.

A few months after Malema became League president, he chose to hand-pick his successor in Limpopo so as to curb Masoga's ambitions. Amid fierce opposition he attempted to install his childhood friend, Jacob Lebogo, as Limpopo's provincial ANCYL leader.

'If Lebogo is not elected, then what brought us together ... is over. And we will meet on the streets,' Malema threatened his peers on one occasion.

It heralded the beginning of a new era. In 2010 Malema eventually got his way: Lebogo was elected as provincial Youth League secretary in what became a highly disputed conference.

Masoga, who was by then the provincial chairman, stood up to Malema for a second time and was one of the first, and certainly the most vocal, to cry foul. Suddenly Malema was in trouble because Masoga's support was significant and it was beginning to swamp Malema's own base in his home province. He chose the most radical option and expelled Masoga from the Youth League, but only after the debacle had been hauled through the country's courts on various occasions.

The ANC leadership turned a blind eye to what was happening and by and large left Malema to his own devices. Of course, this was something they would come to regret before too long, as it gave him a licence to feel even more emboldened than he already was. In his own mind, he was not only the head of the Youth League, but a prominent member of the strong faction that was beginning to reshape the ANC. As far-fetched as that may sound, it was true.

Chapter 7

A political opportunity

Though he is now long departed from their ranks, in an odd kind of way Julius Malema will always remain with and within the ANC, if only as a reminder of how it all went so horribly wrong. Or perhaps it is fairer to say 'when' rather than 'how', because Malema was merely the symptom of a bygone era that the ANC has yet to acknowledge fully. If the time ever does come when they look back at their record as a ruling party in any kind of honest and meaningful way, they will point not to Malema but to the early 1990s and the return from exile when the calamity became truly irreversible.

As history has well documented, the ANC fought a remarkable fight against the apartheid regime that was installed some thirty-five years after it was founded. In its time it produced heroes such as Oliver Tambo, Walter Sisulu, Ahmed Kathrada and Nelson Mandela, the last who went on to become an icon like no other. The organisation spread its fight across the world and its thousands and thousands of ordinary members – both at home and abroad – fought as black outcasts for basic human dignity in ways that, to this day, perhaps have not been fully appreciated.

When the ANC was unbanned in 1990, after thirty years as an underground structure, it began to undergo one of the most

critical transformations of its existence from a secret liberation movement to a would-be ruling party, in keeping with the 'broad-church' concept that had moulded its identity. Even though the political climate was rapidly changing in South Africa and the end of apartheid was now inevitable, there was still a palpable fear associated with black politics after three dark decades of underground life, and taking politics and activism out of the closet again was a huge challenge. It was a process that required critically sensitive leadership and structured political education.

'We used to talk about it in exile when it was becoming apparent to us that we were coming home,' says former government member and long-standing ANC senior Aziz Pahad. 'We knew that managing this concept of the broad church would be difficult once we were back home. We knew it would bring change. But like any change, we would just have to see what kind of change it brought and then learn how to manage it.'

It was a process that would fundamentally change the ANC because what 1990 also brought was a rush on party membership from inside South Africa. While it attracted thousands of individuals who were ready to help take the country to the next level, among the new members were plenty of opportunists laden with the kind of ambition that had little to do with politics. Many who had feared activism throughout the struggle era were now quick to flock to the ranks of the would-be ruling party in the hope of finer things to come.

Former minister in the Mandela and Mbeki governments Sydney Mufamadi put it to me in the following way: 'During the struggle, the cadres had everything to lose and very little to gain by being a member. So people genuinely joined the ANC out of a commitment to their country. But that motivation for joining began to change in 1990.'

Rather than be influenced or changed by the ANC, many of these 'come-lately' members began to change the ANC instead. And the early years after unbanning saw the emergence of a new kind of ANC cadre, the calibre of whom would become a serious cause for concern.

'Since 1991, at the conference in Durban, all the subsequent documents have been picking up on the issue of the calibre of the cadres, be it at policy conferences or general council meetings. It is there. The concerns around the reasoning and values of our cadres are there ... We called it the "decay of the cadre",' Pahad recalls. 'And I often say to people, why are you surprised now? It has been there in writing for a long time.'

Why? Because the process of transformation became an unguided one, unwittingly so, which was perhaps understandable in light of the fact that the ANC was focusing on going into government and preparing to become a ruling party; hence political education and discipline clearly suffered. Compounding the matter was the black business sector, whose members had been at loggerheads with their own communities throughout the struggle era, particularly in the bantustan areas, but who were then quick to align to the ANC post-1990 in a somewhat desperate measure to show they were on the right side of the new political dispensation that was emerging. And, of course, there was the ethnic factor, particularly in a place like Limpopo, which incorporated five of the country's ten former bantustans (Venda, Gazankulu, Lebowa, along with parts of KwaNdebele and Moutse). All factors considered, the governing of Limpopo became a critically delicate balancing act.

It was a province deeply divided by factions of one sort or another from as early as 1994. Ngoako Ramatlhodi, currently a minister in Zuma's government, was premier of that province

from the dawn of the democratic dispensation through to 2004. Throughout that decade he weathered repeated attempts to nip away at his power base, both as premier and as chairman of the ANC in the province. He was succeeded by Sello Moloto, who, like his predecessor, was regarded as a man close to then President Thabo Mbeki. Of course, when the Mbeki–Zuma divide began to play out in 2005, it became particularly acute in Limpopo, where factionalism had become a way of political life.

That Limpopo's political terrain was forever in a state of flux suited Malema, whose politics has always oscillated around a 'them-versus-us' mentality. He had been inducted into the ANC as a fighter and like any fighter he needed an enemy. In 1990 he still had one – the white-led regime and the minority population of white South Africans. As a student activist in the late 1990s and early 2000s, he found his enemy in 'the system' as he fought for transformation in education. From 2004 onwards, he ironically found his enemy within the ranks of his own political party.

Moloto may have been premier of the province, but Malema and Cassel Mathale – then the provincial secretary of the ANC – were in control of the municipalities and many of the party's branches. It was through those dynamics that the two centres of power began to play out. Once again, Malema had his 'them' and 'us', and that divide became even more entrenched in 2005 when the national general council of the ANC decided to support Jacob Zuma's comeback plan. It sparked a wave of anti-Mbeki sentiment all over the country. Malema had a new enemy in Mbeki, but it became less about Mbeki and Zuma as time wore on.

It became a divide not only between nationalists and communists, but between young and old cadres, between the so-called left and right. It unfolded as a new kind of battle for

the ANC, a race among comrades to the top. They pitched their battle as a fight against communism, a battle for the real soul of the ANC, but it was a project of the kind of narrow nationalism and political elitism that the old ANC had warned against as far back as the late 1960s.

Limpopo is an excellent example not only of a real sense of decay within the ANC, but of the kind of political opportunism ideal for a man of Malema's character. The province was under the stewardship of Cassel Mathale, though it was common knowledge that he ran the province with Malema. As surreal as it sounds, Malema was only the ANC's national Youth League leader at the time, but he had an equal say in all of the public contracts that were awarded, business deals that were struck and any other public expenditure worth talking about, much as he tries to deny all of this. Malema had already become a big player in business by then, in both the public and private sectors. With Mathale in his pocket, he was able to feed his bigotry and his greed, which had become two aspects of the same rampant disorder.

Chapter 8

Teething on tenders

It was because of Malema that the portmanteau word 'tenderpreneur' slipped into the South African lexicon half-way through 2009, a pithy if pathetic description for the politics of patronage that had come to define the more entrepreneurial members of the ANC who were increasingly tapping into lucrative state contracts or tenders.

Though not alone in his endeavours, Malema was a master at 'tenderpreneuring' and it was for him that the crude term was created, and hardly a reference was made to him after that period that was not accompanied by it.

By then, his profile was enormous and in many respects he appeared equally as powerful if not more powerful than the state president. There was an invincible air about him, despite that fact that he was only thirty years of age. Perhaps that was the problem: too little life experience and way too much power, a lethal mix that had gone completely to his hot head.

It was this mix that blinded him to boundaries. Possibilities were enormous in his world but he couldn't see that today he might be the big man and tomorrow some kind of hapless hero. He ploughed through life without a care in the world for the repercussions of his words and actions, or the prospect that his excesses would eventually get the better of him.

I recall a conversation I had with Malema in the wake of a heated political moment, sometime late in 2010. I can't remember what it was he had done – no doubt spouted off an insult of some sort. But whatever it was, he found himself walking on the wrong side of the suspended sentence that was hanging over his ANC cap, yet he knew, or at least he thought he knew, he was untouchable among his peers.

'They can't get me,' he said as he laughed heartily. 'I'm the one with the nine lives. They can't bring me down.'

He was ahead of the game at the level of the party, but he was embroiled in a war with the media who were digging into the dark areas of his life and even deeper into his finances.

'Back off' was his standard response. 'I'm a private citizen.' It was the shield he believed made him untouchable in the eyes of the law as well, and which forced him to seek an urgent interdict against *City Press* when it tried to expose his wayward ways halfway through 2011. The newspaper was about to publish some damning allegations and he instructed his legal team to send a senior counsel to the court and argue his corner as a man entitled to privacy. To his dismay, he lost that battle: the court granted the newspaper permission to reveal what had been going on behind the scenes all this time.

In an ironic twist of fate, that same week I had sent Malema an extensive list of questions (which are included in the Appendix of this book) before the first edition of this book was sent to print. A couple of weeks earlier I had met with him to tell him to expect the questions, which would give him his right of reply to allegations the book intended to make.

The questions were drafted by me but sent with a covering letter from the law firm acting for my publisher and myself. And they were hand-delivered to Luthuli House shortly after lunch on Wednesday, 20 July. He was asked to respond within ten days.

Two days later Malema called me, wanting to know if I was behind some of the information that the newspaper had revealed. I wasn't and I told him so.

'This is very suspicious,' he suggested. 'You came here two weeks ago and told me you would send me questions. And now *City Press* does it instead.'

'But surely my questions are not identical to what they might have sent you,' I argued.

'What questions?' he demanded. 'Where are your questions?'

That's when I became aware that he hadn't received them and he quickly sent one of his aides in search of them. I didn't expect to hear from him again, as the letter had instructed him to respond via the lawyers, but that didn't stop him from calling me that same evening.

He had the questions. And he wanted to talk. I appealed to him to liaise with the lawyers directly, as the letter had stated.

'I have some things I want to say to you first,' he said. Here we go, I thought.

He told me he didn't like the fact that I was now communicating with him via a lawyer's letter when I had always engaged with him in person. He reminded me of the extraordinary access I had had to him, which was true.

'You know, for nearly two years you could phone me and meet me and talk to me. And now you end it like this,' he exclaimed.

I reminded him the move was procedural. I told him it was also in his interests; it was his opportunity to set the record straight.

'But why a lawyer's letter?' he wanted to know. 'Why can't we just sit down and talk?'

'You can bring your little notebook and your pencil,' he went on. 'And you can bring a recorder. It will all be on the record. I have no problem answering these questions.'

'So what happens if I raise an issue about some incident or other that you deny, what then?' I asked.

'You stay with your story and I stay with mine,' he responded.

With the lawyer's go-ahead, I took Malema up on his offer and met him in Johannesburg the following afternoon. We met at the upmarket restaurant Wall Street, in the plush business district of Sandton. It was hardly the most obvious choice of venues for a self-proclaimed economic freedom fighter, but it was his choice and over the course of a couple of hours we went through the detailed questions, with the recorder rolling all the while.

What follows is the upshot of that conversation, much of which is the subject of his years-long battle with the South African Revenue Service (SARS) and a pending court case on charges of fraud and corruption. It is something that springs to mind each time I hear him speak about the desperate need for economic emancipation and freedom of the country's swollen underclass; this is the man who cunningly amassed a small fortune, all for himself.

'The ability to make business is one's willingness to go and kick doors,' he told me. 'That's what I have done in the past when I was young.'

He began to dabble in tenders when he was still a teenager and attending the Mohlakaneng High School in Seshego. Malema and his friends competed against the teachers to provide the school uniforms for the few hundred learners and the teenagers won the bid.

'But we underpriced and we didn't make a profit,' he insisted, adding that he didn't influence the outcome in any way. 'I was only at the SRC level then,' he commented, suggesting his powers of sway only came later.

Not long after that he began to rise through the ranks of COSAS and along the way he met Pule Mabe, who was a journalist for the *Mail & Guardian* at the time and was assigned to cover some of Malema's political rallies. Their paths continued to cross when Malema, at the age of twenty, moved to Johannesburg after he became the president of COSAS. That was in 2001 and around the time that Mabe began to give up on the idea of journalism. He secured a stint in the public sector before landing a job at the Passenger Rail Agency of South Africa (PRASA). By then Mabe was involved in many business deals. He and Malema had a lot in common and they established a good rapport (though the two men no longer speak and have long since parted ways).

Malema was like 'Jimmy who comes to Joburg', as Patti Nkobe says of her old friend. He was the farthest thing from a city slicker when he first arrived. And he wouldn't have had the polish or the plush outlook of the rising black middle class either. Mabe wouldn't have been much better. He was another young man from the provinces trying to melt into the metroscape of Johannesburg. Two kindred souls fixed on the city's bright lights. Two of a kind out to make a quick buck.

'Pule at that time was a bit advanced in business,' Malema said. 'He had a Golf, a Jetta, a Combi. And he started introducing me to those types of opportunities.'

But he insisted that it was Mabe who was eliciting most of the tenders and that he was just helping out. He was not involved in all of them, he firmly pointed out. Only a few.

One of those was a tender they won to brand plastic water bottles for Lepelle Northern Water, in their home province of Limpopo.

'This was not me [who got the tender]. Pule came with it. He included me,' Malema said. On that basis, one might assume that

he was brought in to do some work for a fair fee in return. But Malema claimed he did it for nothing: his version was that his toil and troubles did not earn him anything at all.

Another deal that came their way was the coordination of entertainment for the inaugural ceremony of a mayor of the Waterberg District Municipality, in the southern stretches of Limpopo.

'Pule was involved in entertainment,' he explained. 'And we needed to market his company. We were literally knocking on doors from one comrade to the other. That's how we got that tender in Waterberg.'

He cannot remember the year – 'I was still COSAS president at that time' – nor does he remember the amount of money it made for them, though on this one he admitted he did rake some in. I remember him throwing out a figure of R30 000 some time back, but this may not be accurate.

'When the money was paid, I asked Pule to give me his car,' he said. So Mabe pocketed the money and Malema got his first car, a second-hand white Citi Golf.

Quite possibly, there were other business deals that the pair pulled off around that time, but towards the end of 2003 Malema packed up his bags and piled that small Golf high with his possessions and headed home to Polokwane after his term as COSAS president came to an end. That December he was elected as provincial secretary of the Youth League based in Polokwane, but he maintained his ties with Johannesburg all the while.

I wanted to know about the lure of Gauteng and I asked if it had anything to do with the ties he might have developed with the South African Rail Commuter Corporation (SARCC), or indirectly with them through PRASA. The corporation was trying to clamp down on fare evaders – or train surfers as

they were called – and it rolled out the 'Sparapara' campaign to curb the growing trend of non-paying passengers. Through that Malema allegedly won a few tenders on the back of a bid to communicate to the public that train surfing had to stop, tenders that were linked to PRASA, where Mabe was working.

'They were not really tenders,' Mabe had once told me when I talked to him about them. 'I just brought him in to talk to people. I saw him as a voice of reason.'

Malema trotted out the same line all these months later.

'No money,' he said. Just motivational speaking – 'talking to the young ones' – which was in turn raising his political profile. And he casually wrote it off as more of a political project than a moneymaking venture.

'You know, we were suffering financially at that time,' he said. Sello Moloto had replaced Ngoako Ramatlhodi as premier 'and the government was not so available to me. I was not so powerful then.'

We had already hit the spot where he would have to stick to his story and I to mine. He was not far off his twenty-third birthday when he started out as the provincial secretary of the League and despite what he says, friends remember how he began to live life to the full around then, making a name for himself around the city as he scaled the social ladder.

He had started to spruce himself up. Gone were the T-shirts and shorts. Gone were the sandals. The Afro was shaved off. He developed a taste for nice shoes and good clothes and before long an attachment to designer labels. That was also when his waistline began to bulge as he feasted off his new lifestyle. Malema was becoming a new man.

So if there wasn't a second income, where did the money come from to fund it all?

He admitted he belonged to an important clique of key players – 'leading politicians and high business people in the province' – who opened doors for him in all directions. 'We lived like a family. We took care of one another. But no tenders. It was comradeship,' he insisted. 'That's how we are.'

Then I broached the thorny subject of SGL, the firm of consulting engineers that had become infamous through its links to Malema and which, along with one of its directors and another of its beneficiaries, is now being investigated by four of the state's prosecutors for fraud and corruption.

The history of SGL was explained to me in the following way by some people in the know. In 2004, Malema met the two directors of the firm – Lesiba Gwangwa and Jonathan Khedzi – at the home of well-known businessman Matome Sathekge. Sathekge owned Bakgaloka Holdings, and the two men had done some work for him in the past. When they tried to get their own firm off the ground, Sathekge told them Malema would help put some tenders their way. Whatever arrangement they came to would be their own.

Infrastructure projects were plentiful at the time in the province, which was undergoing major restructuring and civil engineering was a good business to be in. But for a young company starting out, with a track record that only spanned a few years, SGL needed a leg-up. And Malema was going to provide it, or so they were told.

Malema flatly denied this.

Sathekge said there was no such suggestion on his part, Khedzi refused to comment on the matter and Gwangwa denied it outright. Malema, however, admitted he was introduced by the well-known businessman to the two young directors, but he said it was for reasons very different from what I had been led to believe.

'What was central in me being introduced to these young chaps was for them to help the Youth League. SGL was donating money to the Youth League programmes,' he argued.

I talked him through the alleged deal as it was explained to me. Malema was to help SGL win tenders and in return he – rather than the Youth League – would earn 10 per cent of the value of each one he put their way. Therefore, the bigger the amount of the tender, the better for Malema. And the more tenders he put their way, better still. For the directors of SGL it was a workable agreement. These tenders were crucial for their growth and survival.

I was told that the brokering fees were allegedly paid out in one of three ways: in cash; in cheques made out to one of his cousins, often Tshepo Malema; or in cheques made out for cash. The cheques would either be collected by his cousin or cashed on Malema's behalf by one of the directors who would then deliver the cash to him. Sometimes he would collect the cash himself, though the pickup point would rarely be at the office.

'How would I do that?' Malema asked.

'You tell me,' I said in response.

'You should have asked the fools who told you to explain [it],' he shot back.

The sources stuck to their guns – that's how it was, they insist, though Gwangwa won't entertain it for a moment. Nor will Malema, who said that even if he had wanted to the political climate was not conducive to it at that time.

'The doors were closed,' he said, explaining that he was on the wrong side of Moloto and times were lean.

'So no tender kickbacks?' I asked. 'No cash payments or cheques made out for cash but for your benefit?'

'No, no, no.'

I recalled a conversation I had had with him in the spring of 2009. We were talking about his lifestyle and when I asked him

what or who was footing the bill for it all, he told me his ANC salary was. He led me to believe that at the time he was taking home something in the region of R40 000-plus a month, when the various deductions were totted up. It was inconceivable that that amount could sustain Malema's lavish ways, though he insisted at the time, 'I don't have any other income. This is it.'

So when his business interests began to trickle into the public domain towards the end of that year, I asked him in which field he felt he excelled: politics or business.

'Do the two have to be mutually exclusive?' he asked in response.

'That would depend on the nature of the business,' I replied.

But even with the correct separation of interests, did he feel he was a better politician or businessman?

'I'm a good deal broker,' he answered. 'That's what I am.'

I reminded him of that conversation as we tried to get the record straight and I turned to the other companies to which he has been linked and on behalf of which he is alleged to have helped to drum up business deals, according to former associates. I asked again if it was possible that there was a budding broker in him all this time.

'You know, in that process there was a point when one registered companies in his name and tried to do some jobs and was not successful' was his careful response. 'And the companies became dormant.'

Was he not a shareholder in Ever Roaring Investments?

'Ja, but I was not always there,' he said.

I asked whether he and his fellow shareholders ever ventured into a multimillion-rand deal linked to Vuna Health Care (which in turn was linked to ANC-owned Thebe Investments) to provide medical supplies across the province over a three-year period.

'I don't know if they had a business with Vuna,' he said in reference to Ever Roaring. 'I never did.'

I put it to him that the deal allegedly earned him – and the other three main shareholders who were with him in Ever Roaring Investments at that time – some R250 000 between them. The tender should have earned them far more, but they scuppered the chance of that at the bidding stage.

He denied this, saying, 'There have never been financial benefits coming from Ever Roaring. It actually took money from us.'

The same applied for Blue Nightingale Trading 61, he suggested, the company to which he appointed himself as a director and some family members as fellow directors.

Yet it was through this company that he secured a 3 per cent shareholding in Tshumisano Waste Management, the consortium that won a R200 million public tender in 2005. Though it had been reported that Malema was bought out a year later, I put it to him that my information showed that he remained as a shareholder until the five-year deal wound down in 2010, the books for which are now being settled.

'Definitely not,' he said, arguing that he wasn't a director of Blue Nightingale in 2005 when the tender began (though I pointed out that would not necessarily preclude his involvement as a shareholder).

In addition to his dividend payouts, my information is that Malema received a payout from the consortium in 2006 that was just shy of R270 000, which financial insiders claimed was a loan, but which in practice was essentially a financial gift.

'What loan?' he asked. 'I don't owe anybody.'

If not a loan, then perhaps a gift, I suggest.

'No' was the flat response.

He was equally adamant that Blue Nightingale was not involved in Beta Projects and the consortium that won multiple and hugely lucrative cleaning tenders throughout Limpopo in recent years. Then I told him I had the financial records that showed a 10 per cent shareholding in the Beta consortium.

'But have you seen the money go into my account?' he asked.

I hadn't. But surely the financial statements spoke for themselves?

'No, it's not true,' he said.

I was fortunate to have had access to the company's records or, in the case of SGL and the other companies mentioned here, to have had access to those who were generally 'in the know' and I was satisfied that I knew how the various business deals were done. When the state's probes are concluded, Malema will be hard-pressed to sustain his denials.

What was remarkable about it all was that his businesses and wealth were blossoming at a time when he was on the wrong side of the provincial political divide that had emerged in the ANC. What is evident now, in hindsight, is that Moloto had lost control on the ground and over his municipalities where Malema and his men were making inroads, in business and political terms.

All told, he was becoming a man of many means, but he was also building a powerful political profile as one of the leading figures in Zuma's comeback plan. In the run-up to the party conference at the end of 2008, a friendly businessman advised him that for the sake of some privacy and tax benefits, he should establish a trust, which he named after his son, Ratanang.

In conversation with me, he stuck to the same line he had been trotting out ever since the trust was exposed in the media: it's a charitable trust; it's for the good of society; it's doing no harm; and it's earning him no wealth.

However, he claimed that in addition to himself and his grandmother, there were many other trustees.

'There are people from outside [the family] as trustees,' he said, 'but it remains a family trust.'

Who are they and when were they appointed?

'I'm not going to tell you that,' he shot back.

Is the trust in order?

'The trust is tax-compliant. Because to buy properties, you have to have a tax certificate and pay tax on property as well. So there is no problem there.'

He had a good chuckle to himself when I asked to see the finances.

'Nobody will see the financials of the trust,' he said.

However, he was eventually forced to hand over the financial records to SARS which, along with a number of corporate forensic investigators, has carried out an extensive probe into the multimillion-rand payments made to Malema over the years. By their calculation, he owes SARS R16 million in unpaid taxes, including the penalties that have accrued over the years. Malema continues to insist that the payments made to him were gifts, that he did nothing in return for his benefactors. However, he has now agreed to settle his bill if SARS will in turn lift the sequestration order that is complicating his new life as an MP.

Tokyo Sexwale, a senior figure in what is now regarded as the 'old ANC', is reported to have settled one of Malema's tax bills that apparently ran into millions of rands, though Sexwale denies this. Should that be proven otherwise, or indeed if the SARS inquiry throws further light on the alleged moneymaking racket at the centre of which Malema operated, the modus operandi of South Africa's ruling party would be blown wide

open as Sexwale is a man with strong political and business ties right across the party.

I often wonder how Ratanang Ramohlale will feel when he becomes a teenager and is recognised as the namesake – and the beneficiary – of arguably the most controversial trust fund in South Africa, which by then will likely have been the subject of various court trials for the fraud that appears to have been channelled through its accounts. When the trust first came to light and the state investigations began, Ratanang was about five years old and I asked Malema if his son was aware of what he had done in his name.

'No, he knows nothing,' Malema said, looking more awkward than I had ever seen him look before. He was clearly uncomfortable and within seconds he shifted the topic.

He began talking me through the property investments that started in 2006 when he bought a plot of land in the up-and-coming residential area of Sterpark in Polokwane, which the locals dub 'Tender Park' today. It sits on the lip of a swathe of land on the eastern side of the city that has been earmarked to house the legislature when it is eventually relocated from Lebowakgomo to Polokwane, and which will add to the value of the area when it does.

Malema bought the site for R222 000 from the municipality, but in a deal that was ironed out in the following way. A friend of his called Matane Mphahlele – the advocate whose name later surfaced in a scandal of alleged company hijacking by the official company's register CIPRO – bought the site in August 2006 for R222 000, though he did not register it until the following April. Once he did, however, it was immediately re-registered in Malema's name.

What was odd about the deal was that the price didn't change when the site changed hands. Is this not a tad suspicious? I asked Malema. Was he not effectively buying off the municipality but shielding such a move by putting Mphahlele up front?

'No, the municipality was about to take the site from him' when Mphahlele failed to raise the funds to secure the purchase. 'And I said give it to me, and he agreed. And I went to the municipality and said, "I'm going to pay the land for Matane, but it must be a double transfer." They said, "No, this is his site. And it must be like he is paying for this site and then he can legally transfer it to [me]."'

If what Malema said is true, then the response on the part of the municipal staff raises questions. The double transfer also sounds odd, if not illegal, and I told him that it was as if Mphahlele might have deliberately defaulted so that Malema could make his move, secure the site at the same low price, but save himself some of the scrutiny about securing prime municipal land as a rising political figure.

But he rejected that notion outright.

He told me he took out a loan from Standard Bank to buy the site, which was then sold on his behalf by a real estate agent a few months later for R680 000. How much Malema actually got for it he will not say. But with the proceeds he put down a deposit on a modest house in Flora Park, for which he paid close to R1 million, rolled by a bond – which has since been cleared – and he immediately pumped a further R500 000 into the house in renovations.

He had the existing walls around the perimeter raised quite high for privacy. He installed a swimming pool and a lapa for entertainment. He changed the windows throughout the house and he renovated the front entrance.

When Malema won the presidency of the Youth League in 2008 he moved back to Johannesburg. He had a short stay in a Sandton penthouse. He then moved to a house owned by Lembede Investments. In April 2009 he moved to a three-bedroomed house in Sandown, the rent on which was R18 000 a month.

The owner, Kenneth Hollingsworth, was approached by a real estate agent who told him she had a tenant who wanted to rent it.

'He's a good tenant. And he will pay cash up front,' she told him.

'Great,' Hollingsworth said.

'You won't have any problems with him,' she continued.

'Great,' he said again.

'Would you have a problem if the tenant was Julius Malema?' she asked.

'Not at all,' he said. 'I don't care who it is so long as it's a good tenant.'

True to his word, Malema paid cash up front for the rental for the entire year, complete with the two months' deposit. The payments came in a couple of tranches.

'I approached Pule and different comrades and asked them to help me pay the rent,' Malema explained when I put it to him the afternoon I sat with him to go through the questions. 'We asked for upfront payments so that we don't go around every month knocking on doors.'

But two months after Malema moved into the house, he decided he wanted to buy it. It was in an ideal location, in a quiet residential estate just off the N1, accessible both for work in downtown Johannesburg and to the N1 to go north to Polokwane. It was surrounded by high walls, which appealed

to him for security reasons. It was neither the mansion nor the luxurious pad it was often portrayed as in the media, but instead a modest-sized home though with ample room for expansion. There was also ample room for parking, which he liked.

So he put pressure on the owner until he relented.

'The house wasn't for sale,' Hollingsworth told me. 'But he wasn't giving up. So in the end, I put a figure on it that was way above the market rate.'

At the time, the house was worth about R2.8 million but Hollingsworth put a price of R3.6 million on it, which Malema immediately accepted.

Again he said he asked for contributions to help him put down a deposit. 'And then they started contributing.'

I asked who 'they' were, but he refused to say.

I told him I had heard there were four men who contributed to the down payment.

'No, different people,' he said. 'There were more than four.'

The one name that kept coming up is that of Tokyo Sexwale. And I asked Malema if Sexwale was one of those behind the house or funding his lifestyle.

'Tokyo – he has never given me money,' he said.

'Has he ever given the trust money?' I asked.

'No, Tokyo has never given the trust money.'

So why does his name keep coming up?

'They try to discredit me by saying I've been bought by Tokyo.'

All my attempts to reach Sexwale were in vain.

With or without him, Malema continued to build his property portfolio. A year later the trust bought a farm in Palmietfontein, on the outskirts of Polokwane. According to the deeds records, it was a cash purchase for R900 000. Not long after that the trust

purchased another property, a residential home in Polokwane, where his son, Ratanang, and the mother of the child, Maropeng, lived for a while.

That house was purchased through Gwama Properties, of which Gwangwa is the sole director but in which the Ratanang Trust has a shareholding. Gwama was the name they created by blending Malema's and Gwangwa's surnames.

Another property, in Quinn Street in Polokwane, cropped up a few months later. I asked Malema how many more might follow and he told me there might be some more. And he left it at that.

He was most certainly cash-rich around that time and was ploughing his money into his property. His wealth was conspicuous in other ways, not least through his cars. From the Citi Golf he drove home to Polokwane in 2003 he upgraded to a white Colt double cab later that year. Then he bought a black Audi 3 series.

'And I had to raise money for that too,' he told me. 'My car subsidy as secretary-general was not enough to cover it. So I asked the comrades to help me.'

Not long after that, he was driving a top-of-the-range black Audi A3 Quattro 3.8. Around the middle of 2008, he bought his first Mercedes. A superior Mercedes followed a year after that. As 2011 started out, Malema took possession of another sleek Mercedes, this time an S600 V12, top-of-the-range model.

In the meantime, other cars featured among Malema's possessions, mostly Land Rovers and Range Rovers. One belonged to businessman Raymond Matume.

'What's wrong with that?' Malema asked. 'We are comrades. He's a businessman. He gives lots of money to the ANC.'

What about the political favours this begs?

But Malema insisted it is not he who doles out the tenders. He might have been a public figure, but at this stage he was not a public official.

Other cars that have featured in the mix have belonged to Lesiba Gwangwa, the director of SGL.

'Lesiba is a friend. He can help me if he wants.'

But Lesiba is also a business partner and a director of a firm that has secured a number of public tenders since Malema began to feature in his life in 2004. In 2010 the Public Protector was called upon to investigate SGL and the possibility that Malema's involvement in it was influencing the multiple tenders the company was winning.

What Advocate Thuli Madonsela concluded was that as far as she could gather, there was no real evidence pointing to irregularities in the tenders. She pointed out that Malema had only joined SGL a year earlier and during his tenure as director, the company had been awarded only three public contracts.

Though Madonsela felt there was no good reason to believe that SGL would not have won them without Malema's involvement, she also acknowledged that much of the paperwork required to carry out the investigation could not be found. And with some minor recommendations about record keeping and transparency, the chapter was closed.

'I denied it,' Malema said when I asked about his directorship. 'I don't know how my name got there … That's what I said. And that's what it was.'

Which, a denial of the truth or a statement of fact?

'Yes. The issue ended like that. My directorship was not confirmed by me. There was never any other issue.'

Yet he openly admitted to having a shareholding in On-Point Engineers (Pty) Ltd, which is held by the trust.

'I've got a relationship with On-Point from a family business point of view, not as an individual,' he said, though he refused to declare the level of shareholding and denied any allegations that he influenced the many tenders the company had been winning.

'I do not know what happens at On-Point. I just queue when the dividends are due.' Then he quickly corrected his slip adding, 'And not me, the trust does that.'

It was the first indication that Malema was directly trading off the public purse. As a result of that revelation, On-Point is now the main focus of the four state forensic investigations into his financial affairs, as the company had won a lucrative tender at the Department of Roads and Transport in 2009. The company was appointed to administer all of the department's public tenders over a three-year period, effectively controlling expenditure to the tune of R3 billion. Documentation that I was given, which listed all the companies that had been awarded contracts, showed how On-Point favoured all of the usual political suspects in the province, and even awarded tenders to itself.

The kickback agreements were quite sophisticated and in some cases drawn up on legally binding documents highlighting demands on the part of On-Point in excess of 20 per cent, but in one case fetching as much as 70 per cent, of the tender amount.

The young man who was tied into that particular deal was a civil engineer working at On-Point, drawing a mediocre salary. With the work that passed over his desk, he could see that a lot of the companies were not sufficiently qualified or experienced to be involved in the kinds of projects they were. Often it was the case that he would do the drawings for them or assist in other ways. Eventually he asked his boss if he could also 'have' a tender. Gwangwa agreed, but demanded a 70 per cent stake. If that's what it took, then so be it, the young engineer thought.

It was stomach-churning to think that seven years earlier, when he forged ties with Malema, Gwangwa was allegedly paying a 10 per cent kickback in 'commissions' for any work brought his way. By 2012 the tables had turned and he was demanding a 70 per cent cut.

By then all of the country's media houses were on Malema's tail and probing his rising fortunes and the fortunes of those around him. Granted, the focus was very one-sided but Malema had come to represent the worst of ANC politics, and though he wasn't the only one draining the public purse dry, the spotlight was fixed firmly upon him. He also gave good mileage as there seemed to be enough damning evidence to satisfy all of the newspaper houses for a number of months, each with its own exclusive take.

At the same time as these exposés were gaining ground, the ANC was attempting to introduce a punitive media bill that would prevent the publication of similar kinds of stories in the future. The Sunday newspapers in particular, along with the *Mail & Guardian*, report excellent forensic-like investigations with a frequency that I doubt exists anywhere else in the world. The sad irony is that it is the endemic culture of corruption in South Africa that has transformed many of the country's journalists into some of the top investigating reporters anywhere in the world.

Yet despite the public glare, Malema continued to live as he had always done. The cash flow remained steady and at the beginning of 2011 he razed his Sandown home to the ground and started to build a luxurious home in its place, at a cost of R8.5 million (though work came to an abrupt halt early in 2012 as the state investigators began to close in on Malema).

Around the same time, his grandmother's home was demolished and in place of the small bungalow a two-storey house rose up.

Yet Malema was becoming increasingly difficult to find on paper, operating instead in what he thought was the safety of the Ratanang Family Trust and elsewhere.

'But it's not a secret trust,' he said. 'It's private.' And another outburst of hearty laughter followed.

Though usually quite cunning, Malema was foolish, if not naive, in this regard. The arm of the state eventually got the better of him, and within the space of a few years he had lost his property portfolio, the proceeds of his trust, his home and, above all else, his standing in life that had afforded him such cheap access to wealth. Malema was bankrupt, financially and politically.

Chapter 9

Fear and loathing in Limpopo

Not long before his fall from political grace in the ANC, Julius Malema was a man-child living like an aristocrat, enjoying his colourful life to the full. He mingled with powerful people and moved in all the right circles. He was paraded about town with his bodyguards in tow. He had drivers who drove his expensive cars – some of which were his own though mostly they were gifts or were on some kind of favourable loan. He was a flashy young thing who wore all of the sleek international brands that feature in glossy magazines. He was dressed by some of the country's top designers. He threw wild and raucous parties at his homes in Johannesburg and Polokwane and plied his guests with French champagne and expensive whiskies and turned his 'house' music up full blast. He liked to be the DJ but when he wanted to get down and dirty, he would hire a music mixer and party hard until the sun came up.

It was fun and frolic for many years and his peers were in awe of him. He was powerful and he was wealthy; in the eyes of his many admirers he epitomised the black man who had finally arrived. In addition to the properties were the acres of land he added to his name, a name that was linked to an array of deals all of which played out alongside his political career that was going from strength to strength. He was the latest thing out of Africa.

But Malema was far too conspicuous for his own good. He was leading a life no different from that of many other prominent cadres of the ANC, the 'new' and 'old' alike. He just lacked the kind of discretion necessary to ensure he could keep it going. So when the lid was eventually lifted, Malema carefully reminded his party peers that he was not on his own. And in the weeks following his financial showdown, he went viral on radio call-in shows and other media outlets to present himself to the world as a product of the ANC, throwing his hands up in the air as if to say, 'What have I done wrong? You taught me how to do it.'

As the world looked on to see how he might talk his way out of his new predicament, millions of Limpopo's residents were clapping their hands in hearty appreciation at the prospect of Malema going down and the hope that it might put an end to the style of governance that had crippled the province in the space of a few short years.

Trumped up though it might sound, Malema was running Limpopo from his Sandown home. Certainly all the right structures were in place to govern the province, but he had put all his men and women in the positions that mattered most and he had a premier – who was both a personal friend and political ally – who was amenable to his ways. Like a traditional chief, it was Malema who called the shots and it was on his watch that Limpopo found itself on rocky ground.

Not long after Malema's fall followed Cassel Mathale's, though he was afforded a softer landing than his prodigy and was sent to parliament in Cape Town. A gross insult, you might think, to a fine institution, but ANC insiders insist the move was always intended to ensure they could keep Mathale onside while the investigations into Malema's affairs ran their course. Even so, it doesn't take away from the fact that during his term there

was a spectacular rise in corruption, and possibly graft, right across the province, which is mineral-rich but desperately poor in socio-economic terms.

If provincial gross domestic product (GDP) per capita were the deciding factor, the province would rank among the poorest in the country, but it would not languish at the very bottom of the pile. But poverty in itself is a big word and if it were taken in its broadest sense, to include an erosion of rights, security, dignity, and so on, in addition to economic deprivation, then the provincial rankings would alter pretty rapidly. If the cost of corruption, poor governance and political factionalism were to be factored in, Limpopo would most likely fare the worst province of them all.

It is all but impossible to put a figure on how heavily corruption weighs on the lives of the province's folk or on the provincial purse. But consider for a moment the structure of the province and then it is easy to see how quickly corruption can take hold.

Government services is the second biggest sector of the provincial economy, after mining, and contributes in the region of 15 per cent to the provincial GDP. Construction, often an indicator of economic growth, is the smallest sector, followed by agriculture and manufacturing, which contribute around 3 per cent each to the total value of production, according to Glen Steyn, a local economist who compiles most of the provincial data. All told, the dependence on government rather than the private sector appears sharp in Limpopo.

And therein lies the danger political analyst Moeletsi Mbeki so often warns of when he says that as a nation, South Africans consume too much and produce too little.

Government – municipal and provincial – is also the biggest employer by far, particularly in Polokwane, the seat of local and

provincial government. The public sector salary bill currently swallows close to two-thirds of Limpopo's annual budget, while it is estimated that a similar percentage of the workforce is employed by government.

In a province with a low rate of manufacturing and production, the government budget is looked upon as a big revenue spinner and the competition for public tenders is high, a situation that makes an ideal breeding ground for graft, something which the Mathale administration is accused of falling prey to.

For as long as Malema was at his peak, the province found itself under intense public scrutiny as the media raked up dirt about one dodgy deal after another involving high-profile politicians and politically connected individuals who were trading on the public purse. But neither the treasury officials in Pretoria nor those in Polokwane can put a figure on the revenue that might have been lost to graft or the percentage of public tenders that might have been negotiated on corrupt grounds. Furthermore, at the end of 2012 the province was declared bankrupt, forcing the national treasury to place it under administration. Despite heavy promises from the then finance minister, Pravin Gordhan, that he would take action against anyone implicated in financial wrongdoing where the public purse was concerned, not a single individual has faced the wrath of the authorities. According to Gordhan's office, twenty-seven forensic reports have been submitted to the Anti-Corruption Task Team for further investigation and twenty-two of these reports sit with the Department of Public Service and Administration so that disciplinary action can be taken, yet not a single head has rolled.

Consider again the Department of Roads and Transport, where Malema was implicated. When Mathale came to power in 2009 he added an administrative layer to the provincial Department

of Roads and Transport, which he called the Programme Management Unit (PMU), and which was then outsourced to a private firm that would effectively administer the department's budget. In other words, the company that would run the PMU would do the work that the department's civil servants had previously done. But by placing it in external hands, he ensured that one single entity would oversee all financial expenditure.

Days before the PMU was put in place a company called On-Point was started by Lesiba Gwangwa, the man who had started SGL many years earlier and who had become a close business associate of Malema's. But by the time it bid for the tender, On-Point was only a few days old. As a company it had no track record and did not possess the skill required. It even went so far as to misappropriate the credentials of one civil engineer who didn't work for the company to ensure it met the technical requirements.

The value of the tender – in the region of R50 million – was not the drawcard, however. It was the fact that the PMU could potentially exercise considerable sway over who gets what deals and when. That was the beauty of it all. I was finally able to establish Malema's role in it all when he admitted that he had a shareholding in On-Point, through the Ratanang Family Trust.

I didn't expect Malema to admit to it. I didn't even know the shareholding was held through the trust. But it was a conversation we had around the time that all of his financial affairs were becoming public and I can only assume he thought it best to tell me about his involvement in one or two of his dealings at least.

Once the On-Point leg was established, the rest fell into place. A list of the companies that had won tenders through the PMU then fell into my lap and with the help of the *Mail & Guardian* investigative team, we put the pieces together.

It was a mess. There was a string of companies headed by people who in one way or another were connected to the city's political elite. There were companies headed by the wives and girlfriends of some of Polokwane's big players, many of them with little or no track record in constructing roads, building bridges and patching potholes.

Not only is it potentially fraudulent to trade in tenders in this way, but it doesn't allow for the right people to provide for the badly needed essential services.

SGL – the forerunner to On-Point – was already a case in point. In the past few years the company has been flagged for poor workmanship many times. There was a taxi rank in Sekhukhune that collapsed. There was a water reticulation system, also in Sekhukhune, that went so badly wrong it cost many times the amount of the initial contract value to put it right, without any repercussions for those responsible.

'It's a phenomenon that has become widespread across the country,' says Sydney Mufamadi. 'Those who don't have the skills or the entrepreneurship to produce are buying access to politicians so that they can access the tendering system that way. And our society is not only becoming one that consumes, but we are now in the early stages of a dangerous kleptocracy.'

Limpopo is also a province that attracts a lot of overseas aid money, yet two diplomats – one from Europe and the other from Latin America – felt that, particularly during the Mathale-Malema era, they could not spend the amount of money they would have liked to in the province because the accounting structures were not in place. Once again, it was those at the bottom of the pile, in most need of development aid, who lost out.

Of course the fiscus also suffers in a climate of rampant corruption, though many will try to insist otherwise. They argue

that if a bribe is paid, it does not affect the tender amount in any way. It is merely a transaction between two people – like a fee – that has no bearing on the cost of the tender or the public coffer that is awarding the contract and it therefore becomes a private arrangement.

That's an argument that is a tad too convenient. In an incident where a bribe has been paid, the person on the receiving end is unlikely to declare it to the taxman, as it is obviously an inexplicable source of income.

It's a dark and dirty world in which anything is possible. A company I have referred to elsewhere in the pages of this book found itself in a tight spot when it became embroiled in the practice of paying out tender kickbacks. Like any company doing business with the state, it was registered for tax purposes and therefore was obliged to declare all payouts over a certain amount to SARS. But the firm of accountants employed by the company in question was unable to settle the company's books. The accountants could make neither head nor tail of the payouts that frequently appeared or the gaping holes cropping up when the payouts were not declared. When they demanded explanations, the company was unable to offer any. The accountants eventually refused to audit the company's books.

However, bribes, fees, payouts and donations, or whatever one might call them, are not always paid in cash or cheques. Matome Hlabioa struck up a friendship with Mathale around the time of the Polokwane conference in 2007, when it became evident that the political ground was shifting and when the would-be provincial leaders began to emerge. He was of the view that five years of friendship could be worth millions in tender revenue and he did what it took to cement the alliance.

It often meant funding parties, not only for Mathale, but for Malema and some of their close associates. Sometimes he would be asked to buy expensive alcohol. On several occasions he picked up the tab for clothes at a boutique in Polokwane. He unashamedly admits that he gave Malema one of his Range Rovers. In essence, Hlabioa was a generous benefactor who never said no.

He and Mathale eventually bought a guest house together on the outskirts of Polokwane and though it was Hlabioa who allegedly put up the capital, they eventually became equal partners in the deal. To balance the partnership and increase his equity in the property, Mathale allegedly channelled tenders to Hlabioa. It was explained to me as 'political capital'.

Within the first few months of sealing their friendship, Hlabioa won various state tenders and was invited into a number of deals, yet that 'political-financial' friendship still remains relatively shrouded in secrecy.

It is often hard to credit the scale of the unashamed plundering that went on during that five-year period and the manner in which the provincial leadership, from Mathale to Malema right down to senior civil servants, could extend their iron fists, and the way in which the officials in Pretoria tended to look the other way.

'But you know you've got a real problem with corruption when those in the know, those at the top, sit back and do nothing about it,' John Githongo, the fearless Kenyan whistle-blower, told me.

For a number of years he had kept careful watch over Nairobi's administration as an anti-corruption fighter and in 2002, when Mwai Kibaki came to power on an anti-corruption ticket, his administration asked Githongo to come into government and help fight graft from within.

Though initially reluctant, he eventually agreed only to be sorely disappointed soon after when he realised the rot was continuing rather than being rooted out.

'But, John, it's our turn to eat,' one of his government peers told him when he began to ask some difficult questions. It was said to him in a tone that suggested he should have known better, that his disquiet was perhaps unreasonable, if not naive.

That was when he decided to begin to root out corruption himself, and over the course of a few months he gathered incriminating information until he had enough damning evidence to blow the whistle on one of Kenya's biggest scandals. His story became the subject of a book by Michela Wrong that bore the apt title *It's Our Turn to Eat*.

'When you know corruption exists, and you know that the chiefs know, and you know that they know you know, yet they look the other way, then you've got a serious problem,' he continued in our interview. 'Because the message that is coming from the top is that it's OK. And that kind of message that can do big damage in a society, it can rip a society apart. That's when corruption becomes difficult to root out, very, very difficult.

'And that's when society forms its own perceptions, and that too can be dangerous. People will expect the worst and will begin to see corruption and graft both where it exists and where it doesn't. They will begin to lose trust in the officials, in their ruling party. And then everything becomes difficult.'

I recall in the run-up to the 2010 Fifa World Cup how the locals in Polokwane used to joke about the African soccer fans who would be travelling to the South African matches from various parts of the continent by land, and how they could surely be forgiven for thinking they were still in Robert Mugabe's country when they crossed over the border at Beitbridge, such was the deterioration of their province and their lives at that time. It was a sad attempt at satire.

Turning and turning in the widening gyre
The falcon cannot hear the falconer;
Things fall apart; the centre cannot hold;
Mere anarchy is loosed upon the world,
The blood-dimmed tide is loosed, and everywhere
The ceremony of innocence is drowned;
The best lack all conviction, while the worst
Are full of passionate intensity.

Surely some revelation is at hand;
Surely the Second Coming is at hand.
The Second Coming! Hardly are those words out
When a vast image out of Spiritus Mundi
Troubles my sight: somewhere in sands of the desert
A shape with lion body and the head of a man,
A gaze blank and pitiless as the sun,
Is moving its slow thighs, while all about it
Reel shadows of the indignant desert birds.
The darkness drops again; but now I know
That twenty centuries of stony sleep
Were vexed to nightmare by a rocking cradle,
And what rough beast, its hour come round at last,
Slouches towards Bethlehem to be born?

(W.B. Yeats, 'The Second Coming', 1919)

Chapter 10

The second coming

Left to his own devices, Julius Malema was ushering a new chapter into South African politics, ironically as the ANC was about to celebrate a century of struggle politics. But Malema belonged to a new generation, one that still relished the thought of a bloody revolution, and he was part of a growing section of society hell-bent on fighting a war that ended quite some time ago, one that was settled through negotiations rather than a bullet.

Though there is a degree of romanticism attached to Malema's induction into the ANC while he was still very, very young, it is important to remember that his earliest instructions were to fight, to attack, to take up arms, the only real solutions that were explained to him then as a means to end apartheid. In his mind, he was plucked from a life of poverty and misery and drawn into a small secret unit of want-to-be soldiers who would have marched into the country's streets in the event that armed resistance became necessary. Even if there is more fantasy than fact to that story around his early years, it is how he sees himself, how he understands the way in which the door of politics swung open for him, why he was 'being called upon' to enter the ranks of a liberation movement, to take to the streets of South Africa and carry on with the National Democratic Revolution.

Apartheid ended with the first free and fair elections in 1994 that followed a series of sensitive negotiations over the space of two years. The Convention for a Democratic South Africa (CODESA) was a forum that brought nineteen political groups to the table to try to thrash out a peaceful end to the regime, but the talks collapsed halfway through when forty-six people were killed in the bloody Boipotong massacre, a reminder of the delicate balancing act the two sides were attempting. The talks resumed on the back of a compromise: a sunset clause that would ease the transition from white minority rule to democracy through a coalition government, essentially an assurance to whites that there would be no backlash from the black majority.

Though the compromise was only ever meant to avert a bloodbath at the time, there are many black South Africans who now feel that too much was ceded in the 1990s, the consequence of which is a white-dominated economy and a society that is still skewed in favor of minorities. They believe that only a revolution would have truly overhauled the institution that was apartheid. Malema is chief among that cohort and to this day he tries to re-enact the war he feels he missed out on.

I remember him once getting some of that sentiment off his chest when he began to articulate some of his pent-up anger and resentment. It never made much sense to me, because Malema had just entered his teens when Nelson Mandela became South Africa's first democratically elected president, promising his people that 'never, never and never again shall it be that this beautiful land will again experience the oppression of one by another' as he was sworn into office in 1994. It was over, apartheid had ended, and though the success of the immediate future would depend on the delicate balancing act of the transition, and would take time – a lot of time – Malema's generation had a lot to look forward to.

Furthermore, it was up to the ruling party, then Malema's political home, to make the changes that were required. Yet in his mind, then as now, is the strong feeling that those who had opposed the new South Africa had been given too light a sentence through the CODESA talks, to which he and others would not have agreed. He is still bitter that he never had a chance to pull the trigger.

'We weren't around during the negotiations,' he told me, his voice a deep growl. 'But we are here now.' And twenty or so years on, he wants change.

As philosopher Achille Mbembe puts it, for certain segments of black South Africa there is a problem with not having won the war through the gun. 'There's a feeling of castration that comes from the idea that we couldn't terminate this war with a bullet and put the whites down by stamping our boots on their throats, as was the case in Zimbabwe. And Malema's war envy suggests he wanted that and almost still does. It's what feeds this kind of lumpen radicalism that has always been a part of South African political culture, but it is now found moving from the margins to the centre.'

Days after Malema's presidency of the Youth League was confirmed in 2008, he addressed a rally on 16 June to mark Youth Day. With a general election only nine months away, the national focus at that time was on Zuma's corruption charges, which were being challenged in the country's courts. It was Malema's first public appearance as president and he wouldn't get a second chance to make a good first impression. He stepped up to the microphone and in a rasping voice told the tens of thousands of youth gathered in front of him that he would not only die but he would 'kill for Zuma' if the charges were not dropped. That was his introduction to the South African public, his first

big sally as youth president. It was a statement that best summed up Malema – he wanted a fight.

A whole anthology of political outrage now survives his six and more years in national politics, each one worse than the last. On the subject of rape, he tried to defend Zuma, who had been tried for raping the daughter of a family friend in 2005, and though Zuma was acquitted, the public jury has kept an open mind on the matter ever since.

'The woman stayed until the sun comes out, requested breakfast and asked for taxi money. She must have had a nice time,' Malema said a couple of years later of Zuma's accuser. For that utterance he was hauled before the Equality Court for hate speech and found guilty.

His most hateful words were directed at Helen Zille, the white leader of the Democratic Alliance and then premier of the Western Cape.

'You have put a cockroach in cabinet and we need to remove that cockroach by voting the ANC into power,' he told an all-black gathering in Zille's home province.

The awful shame in Malema's words related to the 1994 Rwandan genocide in which 800 000 people were killed in the space of 100 days, the majority of them Tutsis who were referred to as 'cockroaches' that had to be 'exterminated'. The minority Tutsis had a monopoly on power in Rwanda, precisely the point Malema was trying to make about the white-led government in the Western Cape. When he was pressed on the matter in parliament, the former Deputy President Kgalema Motlanthe brushed Malema's words aside as 'just downright simple bad manners'.

That was in 2010 and, a year later, at the height of local government elections and while sharing a stage with Zuma,

Malema told his followers that whites were 'criminals' and demanded that they 'must be treated' as such. Zuma didn't possess the civic fortitude to stand up to him so he threw his head back and laughed while the crowds cheered Malema on. Not a word was whispered about the incident until the ANC recorded a drop in minority voters and then all party officials turned their glare on Malema. But the horse had already bolted by then.

As he began his second term as League president in June 2011, and when he was feeling more emboldened than ever, Malema called on his youth following to go to war with the ANC. He was at his peak now and did as he pleased. It was as if the carnival had come to town and was choosing not to leave.

The theory of the carnival, as explained by Russian literary theorist and critic Mikhail Bakhtin, is particularly appropriate here: 'Carnival is not a spectacle seen by the people; they live in it, and everyone participates because its very idea embraces all the people. While carnival lasts, there is no other life outside. During carnival time, life is subject to its laws, that is, the laws of its own freedom.'[1]

When the carnival comes to town, the solemnities, etiquettes and formalities disappear and are overtaken by those who normally reside on the fringes of society. The carnival liberates them. It empowers them. For them, hell becomes heaven. Fantasy becomes fact.

'The carnival only lasts for a short while,' says Mbembe. 'It is a small window of opportunity during which everything is turned on its head. And in that short space of time, you can swear, and you can fuck and fart and spit and all of that.

'But the problem here is that the carnival has become the permanent. We are now living in a permanent carnival. This is

the last chapter of the transition and this is the point at which we have arrived.

'And the engineer of the carnival was Zuma. Remember he brought the song "Bring Me My Machine Gun". He brought some outrageous activities into the political domain. It was he who brought the carnival to the centre of everyday South African life.'

Halfway through his first term, Zuma woke up to the folly he had brought to bear, but he struggled to rein in his comrades, Malema foremost among them. Zuma had allowed the taste of carnival life to linger a tad too long, and now those he brought with him were reluctant to leave.

'They were saying, we will sit here and we will break the pot. And when there is nothing to eat, then we will fight each other,' says Mbembe.

It's what happens at the carnival, when reality and reason no longer ring true, when fantasy becomes fact and when the likes of Malema can do as he pleases, in politics, in business and in every other aspect of his life.

Chapter 11

The invincible

If the true meaning of Malema was then beginning to emerge, then one of the most memorable examples of it was the drama surrounding his trip to Zimbabwe in 2010. Early that year, when the ANC celebrated the twentieth anniversary of the unbanning of the party as well as the release of Nelson Mandela, Malema decided to resurrect the old struggle song '*Dubula iBhunu*', or 'Shoot the Boer':

> The cowards are scared,
> Shoot, shoot.
> Ayeah,
> Shoot, shoot.
> The cowards are scared,
> Shoot, shoot.
> Awu yoh,
> Shoot, shoot.
>
> Shoot the Boer
> Shoot, shoot.
> Shoot the Boer
> Shoot, shoot.
> Shoot the Boer

Shoot, shoot.
Shoot the Boer
Shoot, shoot.

It was Malema's predecessor in the ANCYL and the man he likes to call his political mentor, Peter Mokaba, who coined the modern-day version of *'Dubula iBhunu'*, which he used to chant at political rallies during the tense years immediately before and after the end of white rule in 1994. But as the country settled into democracy, the song faded into the background and was sung only occasionally until Malema decided to trot it out again.

'Why now?' I asked him at the time.

'Why not?' he answered, with a casual shrug of his shoulders. 'We are in charge now. It's our song. We sing it when we want to.'

Within weeks of him doing so, the country's most notorious Boer, Eugene Terre'Blanche, the sixty-nine-year-old founder of the minority separatist group the Afrikaner Weerstandsbeweging (AWB), was beaten to death by two of his farm workers on Easter Saturday afternoon.

Malema was not in the country when Terre'Blanche met his death, though that didn't stop all fingers pointing in his direction as incitement to the murder. He was in Harare, visiting Robert Mugabe and learning about the nationalisation of Zimbabwe's mines and its controversial method of land reform, and I was with him. The afternoon Terre'Blanche was murdered Malema was on the outskirts of the capital addressing a youth rally, at the end of which he sang *'Dubula iBhunu'*, which he had been banned from singing in South Africa by Pretoria High Court Judge Eberhard Bertelsmann two days earlier. When news of Terre'Blanche's death reached Malema, he was the guest of honour at a gala dinner attended by some five hundred of Zimbabwe's top business people.

The news did little to distract him. He simply proceeded with his schedule. Malema and his Zimbabwean friends were plotting a different battle.

The following morning a VIP motorcade pulled out of the Sheraton Hotel where he and his fellow ANCYL members were staying. The twenty-three-car convoy started out with a visit to some small landholdings in Mashonaland that had been returned through Mugabe's land-reform programme to the local folk to farm. Then they visited a platinum mine owned by Zimplats, a target of the country's indigenisation plan to force foreign investors to cede 51 per cent of shareholdings to black Zimbabweans. The majority of its shares are owned by South Africa-based Implats, along with a 13 per cent shareholding by independent investors, and it is listed on the Australian stock exchange. Its foreign make-up ensures it is a prime target.

Next stop was Harare's main football stadium, where Malema was billed to walk onto the pitch at the start of a game between local top team Dynamos and Lupopo, from the Democratic Republic of Congo. But by the time the convoy crawled through the gates of the stadium, the match was long under way, so the South African youth and their Zimbabwean hosts settled into some VIP seats and watched the game for a while.

Half an hour or so later, the enterprising group was back on the road, headed in the direction of New Donnington Farm in Norton, which is about sixty kilometres south-west of the capital and owned by the country's former controversial Reserve Bank governor Gideon Gono.

In the absence of any other viable farms to showcase, most high-profile visitors to the country are usually taken to Gono's. Spread over an area of four thousand hectares in a district where farm size is limited to four hundred hectares, New Donnington

comprises two farms that were collapsed into one when the governor acquired them some years back.

New Donnington was the last stop of the day and Gono had decided to throw a party in honour of the South African youth. A marquee was erected on the lawns of the main house and as the convoy made its way down the farm's ten-kilometre driveway, the slaughtered beasts were turning tender on the braai.

I was travelling in a car with Pule Mabe, the treasurer-general of the ANCYL, and it was then, as we reached the farm, that Malema's grand plan finally became apparent to me.

'You see, South Africa is the biggest producer of platinum in the world,' Mabe told me. 'Zimbabwe is sitting on big reserves of platinum as well.'

Southern Africa's reserves were discovered in the mid-1920s, but exploration proper only began many decades later as the multiple uses of platinum-group metals became apparent. Industrialists now say that one in every five manufactured items either contains or is produced with platinum, making it one of the most strategic metals in the world. The price of the precious metal had almost tripled from US$500 per ounce in 2000 to US$1 500 by then, 2010.

However, platinum is very rare. Below-surface deposits account for only a minute fraction of the earth's crust, occurring at only 0.003 parts per billion of the total, according to one estimate. Above-ground reserves would only meet a year's demand. A telling fact that mining speculator Greg McCoach likes to point out is that if all the platinum in the world were poured into an Olympic-size swimming pool, it would just about cover one's ankles.

The two southern African countries are sitting on the vast majority of the world's deposits. So large is South Africa's

platinum wealth that it now supplies in excess of 80 per cent of global demand. Zimbabwe's deposits and potential sources are not insignificant, though its production has not been as high as its neighbour's. On the upside, however, what makes Zimbabwe so important for mining houses and investors is the fact that the metal is closer to the surface than it is in South Africa, making operations less costly and profits and returns more attractive.

'So if we can work together, we can create a superpower,' Mabe went on. 'Africa's first big superpower. And then we will be fully independent and we will stand up to the world. Africa can't do that without a superpower.'

His train of thought began to unfold as he told me how easy it would be to pull it all off. He grinned as he snapped his fingers. Malema's revolutionary thinking would capture the African imagination, he believed, and it would build up momentum as it worked its way up through the continent from the southern tip.

There was no talk of sovereignty, or independence, or likely and logical resistance to the grand plan. Just a rousing rendition of why it must happen and how 'we never realised the responsibility we were being given when we were elected as the leaders of this Youth League. But we need ZANU-PF to do it.' And his hosts were giving them all the right signals that night.

Malema, Mabe and his ZANU-PF hosts were seated at a top table in the marquee, facing onto the gathering of about 150 or so guests, the majority of them ZANU youth.

As the evening began to draw to a close, Malema rose to his feet to give his hosts a lecture in political survival. As the youth of ZANU-PF, you may be down but you are not out, he assured them, promising that the ANCYL would help them get back on their feet. But they must be relevant to the people of Zimbabwe – of them, not against them. And if they can become

relevant to the youth of Zimbabwe, then ZANU-PF has a future. Malema warned them against violence. It could have no place in driving their political project. But that did not mean that they must surrender. They simply had to find another means to fight their battle.

'This is war,' Malema told them. 'Arm yourself now, like you did in the past giving us AK-47s to go and fight the regime. But today the struggle is different. You are arming us to prepare ourselves for another confrontation. Because the struggle today is a struggle for economic emancipation. And we shall overcome ... '

They loved his every word and sang and danced at his feet in appreciation as his speech came to a close. There aren't too many people who are prepared to bring ZANU-PF back to life and that Malema had travelled to Harare to throw them a lifeline made him a hero in their eyes, the new big man of Africa.

'The winds of change are blowing across Africa,' Saviour Kasukuwere, Zimbabwe's then minister for youth development, indigenisation and empowerment, said as he took his turn at the podium after Malema stepped down.

'[Your] coming to Zimbabwe has changed the mood of our country ... Your speech tonight is a watershed speech here,' he told Malema. 'This political education will forever remain in their ears.'

Kasukuwere likened Malema to Alfred Rogers Nikita Mangena, the Zimbabwean guerrilla chief who was killed in battle in 1978. He was on his way to becoming the commander-in-chief of the Zimbabwean army, Kasukuwere continued. 'And he was only thirty-three.'

'He is the commander of southern Africa at twenty-nine,' he said, pointing in Malema's direction.

Kasukuwere went on to tell his audience why Zimbabwe needed to regain control of its economy and mineral assets and stop the flow of the country's wealth overseas.

'We need to intervene,' he said. 'And that's why we salute this brave young bull,' he said in reference to Malema.

Earlier in the evening he had told the South African youth leader and the seven ANCYL members who had travelled to Zimbabwe with him that their hosts wanted to give them a gift to mark the 'historic visit'.

'A heifer. For each of you,' Kasukuwere said. That was their take-home prize for befriending ZANU-PF. That's how the Zimbabweans wanted to show their appreciation.

Malema's face was expressionless at first, as was that of Mabe, who was sitting next to him at the top table.

'A heifer. A virgin cow,' Kasukuwere explained to the two city slickers.

'And a bull as well for you, Comrade Julius.'

With that they were marched outside the marquee to a patch of land where the bovines were grazing in a cordoned-off area of grass, waiting to be vetted. They were healthy-looking heifers, but not a patch on Comrade Julius's bull. He was a prize-winning beast and had scooped the country's top awards in 2007, 2008 and 2009 at Harare's Agricultural Show. He had the badges to prove it, all of which were neatly displayed on a small board nearby that was hanging off the fence.

Not to be outdone, Kasukuwere said he would personally match the gifts and pledged to give each of the South African youths a heifer 'as well as a bull for Julius'. Gono agreed that he would do likewise. All told, Comrade Julius would take home three heifers and three bulls, while his colleagues would take home three heifers each.

The underlying message was not to be missed, they were told: the animals were to graze on the land that rightfully belongs to the people of South Africa.

And the bulls were equally symbolic. They were a mark of strength and bravery. 'And you must never behave like a castrated bull,' Kasukuwere told Malema.

March on, he ordered the young South African. And be brave. 'You can shoot Malema tomorrow, but you can't shoot the idea,' he continued. 'Anyone who thinks they can stop Malema, they can't.'

'You are free,' he told Malema. 'That song must be sung. "Shoot the Boer".'

And with that they all got to their feet and sang and danced to the words of '*Dubula iBhunu*'.

The following morning Malema had a meeting with Mugabe at State House and a short while later he flew out of the country, feeling every bit the hero the Zimbabweans were telling him he was. He was the new big man of Africa.

That powerful feeling was still with him when he called the media to a press conference at Luthuli House three days later. Members of both local and international media houses were quick to respond to his invitation. The country was still tense in the wake of Terre'Blanche's murder and though Terre'Blanche and his politics were for most people a throwback to another era, his killing had rocked South Africa to the core and left its racial wounds raw and gaping once again. Malema was standing squarely in the firing line of the latest divide and the media wanted to hear what he had to say for himself.

Yet he was showing few concessions to social or political pressure that Thursday morning as he opened the press conference. Remorse was the furthest thing from his mind.

'He died before changing his racist behaviour,' Malema had said of the AWB leader in the immediate wake of the killing. 'His death should not be linked to the ANC struggle song ... Our hands do not have blood.'

Instead, Malema wanted to brief the media about his four-day trip to Zimbabwe during which he had lauded President Robert Mugabe for his leadership, hailed Governor Gideon Gono as a financial genius for his creativity at the Reserve Bank, and pledged to breathe political life back into ZANU-PF at the expense of their unity government partners, the Movement for Democratic Change (MDC).

Not surprisingly, the MDC was quick to criticise Malema, as a prominent member of the ANC, for taking sides at a time when the South African government, a supposedly neutral neighbour and broker, was still overseeing Zimbabwe's fragile transition.

But Malema ignored what they had to say and instead chose to restate and reinforce his views as the press conference got under way. 'We want ZANU-PF to be retained in power. That's what we want,' he told the media contingent in his opening remarks. 'We are not going to relate with some Mickey Mouse we don't know. We relate with people we've got history together [*sic*].'

'They will never find friendship in us,' he continued. 'They can insult us here from air-conditioned offices of Sandton. We are unshaken. They must stop shouting at us. They must go and fight for their battle in Zimbabwe and win. Even if they've got ground, and they are formed on the basis of solid grounds in Zim, why are they speaking in Sandton, and not Mashonaland or Matabeleland?' he asked.

Once again it was 'them' versus 'us'. If you are not with him, then you are against him. The MDC started out as the enemy that Thursday morning.

'Let them go back and go and fight there,' he went on as he settled into his pitch. 'Even when the ANC was underground in exile, we had our internal underground forces fighting for freedom. And … '

'You live in Sandton,' Jonah Fisher, a BBC journalist at the time, cut in before Malema could get the rest of the words out of his mouth.

What he pointed out was a fact. Within a year of Malema moving to Johannesburg to take up the post as the ANCYL's leader, he had bought himself a home in the northern suburb of Sandown, on the doorstep of the upmarket business-cum-residential area of Sandton.

Why that irked Fisher was not entirely clear, nor was it apparent what it had to do with the MDC. Malema was making the point that some members of Morgan Tsvangirai's party were based in South Africa while there was work to be done on the ground in their home country. Why he didn't point that out to Fisher was poor play on his part. But that's when the fun started.

'… and we have never spoken from ah, ah, ah, ah, exile,' Malema continued, as he stuttered through to the end of his sentence, evidently thrown by the unexpected interruption.

Malema hadn't anticipated Fisher's challenge. His excesses had not only gone unchecked by his own party for quite some time, but the 'big man of Africa' feeling that was endowed upon him in Harare was still with him. He was still on a political high.

'You see, here, let me tell you before you are *tjatjarag*,' Malema said, turning to Fisher, his pudgy forefinger pointing in the direction of the journalist as he leaned across the table that separated him from the media pack. 'This is, this is a building of a revolutionary party and you know nothing about the revolution. So here …'

134

Fisher interrupted him for a second time.

'So they're not welcome in Sandton, but you are?' he asked. Fisher's tone and his line of questioning riled Malema no end. There are not many people who challenge the Young Turk in public and here was a white British male, of all people, ridiculing him in front of the media, of all groupings.

'... so here, here, here you behave or else you jump,' Malema shouted, reminding Fisher in a heavy-handed manner that they were on the eleventh floor of Luthuli House. 'So here you ... '

Fisher cut in for a third time, this time laughing at the young man's ranting.

'Don't laugh,' Malema hollered at him.

'This is a joke,' Fisher responded.

'Chief, can you get security to remove this thing here?' Malema said to whomever of his comrades was standing near the door.

'If you are not going to behave, we are going to call security to take you out,' he said, turning to Fisher once again.

By then the sound of clicking cameras was nearly as loud as Malema's voice as photographers jostled to capture the moment on film.

'This is not a newsroom, this. This is a revolutionary house. And you don't come here with that tendency,' he continued, his finger wagging furiously. 'Don't come here with that white tendency,' he shouted, his voice rising to fever pitch.

'Not here. You can do it somewhere else. Not here. If you've got a tendency of undermining blacks even where you work, you are in a wrong place. Here you are in a wrong place.'

Fisher butted in for a fourth time before Malema's last few words could be heard. 'That's rubbish,' he said as he began to pack up his bag.

'Then you can go out. Ja, you can go out,' Malema said as he watched his new foe prepare to leave.

But as the journalist walked to the front of the room to retrieve his microphone, which was set up right in front of Malema seated at the table, the ANCYL leader decided to lower the tone of the spat.

'Rubbish is what you've covered in that ah, ah, trouser,' he remarked fatuously, pointing at the journalist's genitals. 'That is rubbish. That which you have covered in this trouser is rubbish.'

What Fisher's private parts had to do with anything remains a mystery, but Malema had reached boiling point by then and it was all downhill after that.

'OK?' Malema continued in a provocative tone, as if he were now seeking a reaction. 'You are a small boy. You can't do anything.'

'I didn't come here to be insulted,' Fisher shot back.

'Come out. Go out,' Malema roared, tongue-twisted mid-sentence amid the frenzy.

'Bastard. Go out. You bloody agent!' he shouted at the top of his voice as Fisher walked towards the door.

For a fraction of a second a deathly silence hung over the room. There were no more clicking cameras. No more sniggering journalists. Not even the sound of a single member of the media walking out in solidarity. Just the deafening sound of shock, which was only ruptured a moment or two later when Malema casually proceeded with the event as if nothing had happened, returning blithely to his views on Zimbabwe and why he felt the neighbouring country was a misread success story.

Within minutes of Fisher walking out of the door, the journalist became a news story in his own right while the youth leader quickly earned himself the nickname Kidi Amin as footage of the

sordid drama was uploaded onto websites and social networks all over the world. One of the first of South Africa's post-1994 leaders had just stepped up to the podium and bared his true colours.

I was at home that afternoon and listened to the drama unfold on the radio. A while later I watched the footage on the Internet. I watched it over and over again that afternoon. That evening, as the dust began to settle, I spoke to Malema by phone. I wanted to know why he had done it.

'No, man. You don't get it,' he said.

Perhaps I didn't, but I still wanted to know what could have provoked such an extreme reaction on his part.

It could be argued that Malema was not alone in his bad behaviour that day. Though Malema was undoubtedly the worst offender, Fisher had also stepped out of line. The BBC journalist and all the other members of the media were at the so-called revolutionary house at the invitation of the ANCYL, after all. Malema was giving his spiel about his four-day trip to Zimbabwe and protocol suggested that he should have been allowed to have his say, regardless.

But Fisher couldn't have liked what he was hearing and chose to dismiss the Youth League leader's words mid-sentence, without signalling or excusing his interjection. And in doing that, he touched on a very raw nerve.

Malema's behaviour was wholly unacceptable; still, it's hard to imagine the likes of Fisher adopting the same tone of gusto with senior politicians such as President Jacob Zuma or other cabinet ministers. It is equally difficult to imagine one of South Africa's black journalists addressing the Tory youth leader at Millbank in London with the same kind of bravado and getting away with it. Or, for that matter, Fisher addressing one of his own politicians in the same manner.

All that said, Fisher's behaviour still didn't warrant Malema's outburst. Could he not simply have asked the journalist to leave, I wondered? Could Malema's spokesperson, the unlikeable Floyd Shivambu, who was seated next to him, not have called the house to order? Did Malema really have to get personal with Fisher?

'Why the extreme anger?' I asked.

'You don't know what it's like to have a white man tell me what to do in my own house,' he responded.

There was not a trace of anger in Malema's voice as he explained this. He was reeling after the day's events and was merely putting words to something very heartfelt, something that runs very deep in his thinking.

What happened at 'revolutionary house' that Thursday morning should have sounded the alarm bells in Malema's mind. But if they did sound, he was not about to heed them. He continued to walk a fine line.

It was common knowledge that his party was mulling over whether or not to slap him with disciplinary charges on three counts: defying the ANC's line on Zimbabwe; singing '*Dubula iBhunu*'; and his treatment of Fisher.

Zuma was scheduled to leave the country for a state visit to the United States, from where he would travel on to Brazil. On the eve of his departure South Africa was still firmly focused on what Malema might do next. So Zuma decided to call a snap press conference during which he publicly humiliated the young man by telling the media that Malema's behaviour was 'alien' to the ANC. This was no laughing matter and Zuma left Malema in no doubt about it as he boarded the state jet and headed out of the country.

Sarah Malema was left reeling from Zuma's words. Her grandson must really have stepped out of line for Zuma to speak out like that, she thought. She immediately reached for her phone.

'Tell me, what did you do?' the old woman wanted to know when she got through to her grandson.

He tried to dismiss her question lightly, but she was having none of it.

'You must have done something very wrong for Zuma to speak about you on the television like that,' she said. 'Zuma is a good man. He doesn't fight with people like that.'

'Do you hear me?' she continued. 'You will lose your job. They are going to fire you. Zuma is complaining about you.'

Malema didn't try to challenge his grandmother, but continued to listen.

'You are the first person we know that Zuma is fighting with,' she said in a stern tone.

'Yo,' he thought as the call came to an end. 'This was serious. This woman stood by me always. And she only ever phoned me twice to give out: once about Naledi Pandor and now about Zuma.'

Malema considered her words carefully 'because when I hear her talk like that, that's where you get the feeling of the last ordinary people and how they feel about [what you do].' Granny was a good barometer. And he knew he would have to make up for the lost ground if he was to hold onto whatever popularity he had among the masses.

But Zuma had no sooner left the country than the invincible Malema stepped onto the nearest platform and grabbed a microphone to tell a gathering that Thabo Mbeki would never

have done what Zuma had just done. And in comparing Zuma to Mbeki, Malema had finally crossed the line. Within days he was facing a disciplinary hearing.

Malema did his level best to prevent the charges from sticking and in a subsequent meeting of the National Executive Committee (NEC), he told his fellow comrades why they couldn't possibly charge him for aligning with ZANU-PF. At the Polokwane conference in 2007 the ANC had passed a resolution to extend support to the neighbouring liberation movements, ZANU-PF being one of them.

'I was simply doing my job,' Malema told the meeting. 'Polokwane said we must strengthen [our] relationship with former liberation movements like SWAPO, like FRELIMO, like ZANU-PF. You must have a structured relationship with ZANU-PF,' he told them.

'I then repeated [it],' he told me later. 'I said, "I want to repeat: You must have a structured relationship with ZANU-PF." And then they laughed.'

He then reminded the executive that when he was taking them through their induction as the new NEC in 2008, Kgalema Motlanthe 'said you must learn to protect resolutions of your own conferences'.

'But you were not at that meeting,' some of his comrades pointed out.

That much was true.

'Whatever,' Malema retorted. 'But you know the fact that Kgalema told you you must protect decisions of your own conferences.'

With that, he successfully had that charge quashed as well. It didn't take much effort on his part to point out to the ANC why it wouldn't be a good idea to side with the media.

140

Since coming to power, this new ANC has been hell-bent on silencing the so-called Fourth Estate at all costs.

So the charge for spitting fire at the journalist also fell away. And for all the reasons that would later play out in a courtroom, they couldn't possibly rebuke him for singing a struggle song.

What Malema couldn't wish away was the comparison he had made between Zuma and Mbeki. That was anathema. It was this 'new' ANC that had recalled Mbeki while still a sitting president and it was inconceivable that it could now concede that he may have been a stronger leader than Zuma in some respects. Hence, it was for that benign offence that Malema eventually faced a disciplinary hearing in May 2011.

Before he faced those who were tasked to bring him into line, Malema went home to Seshego, where Sarah slaughtered a goat and performed a ritual. 'First I had the slaughtering and then I went to the DC [disciplinary committee]. That's why I'm still here,' he later told me.

Malema had asked Jeff Radebe to represent him at the hearing. Radebe initially agreed, but then closer to the date withdrew and offered his own lawyer instead.

'But we knew we needed someone with political clout, so we asked Mathews [Phosa].'

Phosa agreed and turned out to provide a solid and excellent defence, but Malema was still found guilty. He was ordered to apologise to Zuma. He was told he would have to attend anger management classes. He also had to pay a fine of R10 000 to a youth development project of his choice. The most damning part was that the disciplinary committee slapped a two-year suspended sentence on him: if he were found guilty of ill discipline again before May 2012, he would be axed from the party.

Malema duly retreated from the public eye for a while. The dust had to settle and he had to rethink his steps. But his silence

must not be misunderstood, he told me when I saw him a month or so later. That he was brought before the disciplinary committee didn't bother him much, he said.

'The disciplinary charges are politics. Politics was coming to me now. It's what I have done to other people before. Now it was my turn. I've always been a problem, so what's the problem?' he shrugged.

He scoffed at the idea of anger management classes.

'It's imposing on me the culture I don't know. In my tradition, if you are angry, they perform a ritual, because it means you have angered the ancestors,' he explained.

Anger management classes don't feature in his world. The fine he could live with. The apology he got out of the way pretty quickly. But the suspended sentence would be a different matter. He would have to be careful now.

What bothered him more than anything though was the fact that he had been let down by some of his comrades, people who had told him not to worry, that there would be no disciplinary charges. Or others who are normally by his side and opted to stay silent throughout the entire saga, not uttering a whisper of support in public when he needed it most.

'I will never rely on an individual again. I should have learned this from Peter [Mokaba],' he told me that day.

I asked him if he regretted his actions. He said it wasn't what he did that he regretted, but what he hadn't done.

'I only regret I didn't put some expensive shoes on his back,' he said, referring to Fisher. 'You know there, I just put politics aside. I saw some young boy who is white, who is demonstrating some white supremacy to me. I wanted to kick him. I was very angry.

'You know, my township character just came out. When you are undermined in the township, you don't negotiate.'

142

It was what he told the leadership of the ANC when he stood in front of them not long after the incident to explain why his temper had gained the better of him that morning.

'That's why in meetings we have tables, to deal with these kinds of problems,' Kgalema Motlanthe told him in jest.

And what about the cows he had left grazing in Zimbabwe? I asked. He laughed in response.

'I will not touch those things,' he answered. 'They got me into big trouble. They can stay there.'

Unable to help himself, Malema continued to court trouble throughout the following year, at the same time as a not insignificant number of Youth League members began to tire of his dictatorial style. By the time he headed for re-election in June 2011, he faced stiff competition but it was never really clear if he could have withstood the challenge as his opponent, Lebogang Maile, withdrew at the eleventh hour. Hence it was a bitter victory for Malema, which might explain the closing speech he gave to the conference and which sent an icy chill throughout the country.

Though he spoke for more than an hour, off the cuff, it was in one mouthful, and a terrifying tone, that he said it all:

'Comrades, there must never be a meeting of the ANC if young people don't constitute 50-plus per cent [of those present] if we want to change this ANC. And by the way, we are not going to win the ANC over through speaking here at Gallagher. We must go to the ground. We are going to war, comrades, a war for radical policy shift.'

It was the kind of rhetoric he stuck to for the next couple of months until the ANC finally chose to part ways with him.

Chapter 12

The Marikana moment

South Africa was still reeling from the gruesome massacre in Marikana when Julius Malema waded into the thick of the tension that Saturday afternoon to preach to the miners and their families. Forty-eight hours had passed since the police had sprayed the workers with bullets, killing thirty-four of them and injuring seventy-eight more in the deadliest show of force since the darkest days of apartheid.

The miners worked for Lonmin, the multinational platinum producer, but had gone out on strike on 10 August when they began to demand a living wage of R12 500 per month. All told, there were approximately three thousand of them who walked off the mine in Wonderkop, a small village about seven kilometres from the mining town of Marikana. The strike action was tense to begin with because the day the miners presented their demands to the National Union of Mineworkers (NUM), the majority union at the mine, they were fired at by union officials and immediately fled to the koppie that sits a stone's throw away from the mine. But the initial tension soon turned to violence when they began to turn on one another in fits of anger, killing themselves, the security guards and the local police, and by the end of the first week of strike action, ten people had been killed, some of them hacked to death and their body parts used for *muti*, or witchcraft.

Though strikes were not uncommon among the blue-collar workforce, what was evident that year – 2012 – was that the workers were no longer prepared to work for the kind of slave wages that underpinned the South African economy. Mining was a big employer and contributed significantly to the country's GDP, but the workers earned poverty-level wages and lived in appalling conditions, either in grim hostels on the mines where there were often six men to a room, or in shacks in the vicinity that were not much better. Their salaries were shameful and had hardly changed an iota in relative terms since 1994, yet the income gap between the workers and their management was breathtaking. In the case of Lonmin, the CEO was earning 211 times what he was paying his lowest-paid worker the year that the strike began, a scenario that only the misguided would have hoped could last.

Two years earlier the Arab Spring had visited the north of the continent when massive social unrest in Tunisia spilled over into Egypt, Algeria, Libya and Syria, and within the space of a few short years dictatorships had been toppled and rulers had been forced from power in a number of countries on the back of a revolutionary wave of protests and riots. Naturally, it prompted talk on the airwaves here about whether or not an Arab Spring might take hold in South Africa, the most unequal country in the world in socio-economic terms. Yet it was a prospect that was always dismissed – and wrongly so, because a revolution was already beginning to unfold here. It simply manifested itself in the form of labour disputes rather than violent street protests.

What was also coming to light in 2012 was the extent to which workers had lost all faith in the ANC-aligned NUM, to which they had belonged for decades but which was doing precious little to lift them out of their misery. This was partly to do with

the inconvenient structure of the tripartite alliance (the ANC, the South African Communist Party and the Congress of South African Trade Unions) that jointly governs South Africa, and though it was a clever and strategic move when it was introduced more than two decades ago, it was a structure that had allowed an all-too-cosy relationship to develop between the unions and the ruling party in the early days of the democracy, to the extent that workers eventually began to lose out as unions pandered to the power of the ruling party rather than to the pressing needs of their core clients, the workers.

What that Lonmin strike also blew wide open was the collusion that had developed between mine owners and senior ANC officials who had been benefiting from the once lucrative mining sector. It was an unintended consequence of the very flawed Black Economic Empowerment (BEE) policy put in place by former President Thabo Mbeki not long after 1994, and though his intention had always been to grow a black middle class, it was a small crop of politically connected individuals who benefited instead.

One such was Ngoako Ramatlhodi, the incumbent mining minister, who since his days as the two-term premier of Limpopo has amassed a fortune as a BEE partner in a number of mining companies. Yet this didn't deter him from attempting to end the five-month platinum strike in 2014 days after being appointed as the mineral resources minister, despite the conflict of interest his business portfolio presents.

Another example is Cyril Ramaphosa, the country's deputy president. When he left active party politics in the late 1990s he turned to the corporate world and became hugely successful and enormously wealthy and was often referred to as the face of South African black capitalism. Through his investment holding

company, the Shanduka Group, he became active in the fields of resources, telecoms, property, energy and financial services, and it was around 2009 that the resources arm of the group became the fated BEE partner of Lonmin, when it acquired control of a company called Incwala Resources.

Hence when the Lonmin strike began to spiral out of control that August, it was Ramaphosa, as the politically connected executive, who was called upon to lean on his government colleagues – among them the then police minister, Nathi Mthethwa, and the then mining minster, Susan Shabangu. He duly did, as would later come to light in a damming email trail between him and his Lonmin peers in which he described the ten killings in the days ahead of the massacre as 'dastardly criminal actions' that called for 'concomitant action'.

Of course it wasn't Ramaphosa who drafted in the police, nor was it he who instructed them to mow down the thirty-four miners. But it was the way in which he, as the ANC BEE man (and incidentally the former head of the NUM as well), appeared so willing to do the bidding on behalf of Lonmin that was most galling to many. That was the deal, though. The likes of Ramaphosa was being milked by business every bit as much as he was benefiting from BEE.

None of the email detail came to light until some time later. In the immediate aftermath of the massacre, the country was too shocked to contemplate anything other than the brutal force used by the police that Thursday afternoon. Even though it was all over in the space of sixty or so seconds, the build-up to it had suggested something was going to happen that afternoon, though nobody could ever have anticipated the slaying of the miners – hence the heavy presence of the media that captured it all.

Police officials had said that morning that 'today is the day that we intend to end the violence' and disarm the miners and remove them from the koppie, but they refused to say how they planned to do it. At around 4pm, they began to concentrate their presence in the area and made repeated calls to the miners to disarm and disperse. They then fired tear gas and water cannons, but the miners remained resolute. The police turned to the media and appealed to them to move back, telling them they could no longer be responsible for their safety. The cameras zoomed in on the helicopter hovering overhead and the Nyalas as they began to roam the area, raising a thick dust from the scrubland. Then they focused on the hundreds of police officers, with their assault rifles cocked, as they advanced towards the koppie in organised droves. The miners, armed with machetes, spears and some guns, initially stood firm. At 4:06pm, the police opened heavy fire and within a couple of minutes a field strewn with dead bodies appeared on TV screens all over the world.

President Zuma was on a state visit to neighbouring Mozambique when it occurred and his delay in addressing the nation, even from Maputo, only added to the consternation. Behind the scenes there was chaos, with Mthethwa returning only a few of his calls, but that still did not explain why it took the president so long to appreciate the magnitude of what had happened at home. He eventually cut short his trip the following day and travelled to Wonderkop to visit some of the injured miners who were being attended to in the small hospital that is owned and run by Lonmin. One of the men took him by surprise when he turned to the president and said, 'You have killed your own people'. Zuma knew then he dared not address the thousands of angry miners who were gathered about two hundred metres away and

he swiftly turned on his heel and headed straight for Pretoria. He had lost control of a very critical situation.

The president was not alone, however, and with the possible exception of General Bantu Holomisa of the United Democratic Movement, there was not a single political leader who could have addressed those miners in the wake of the massacre. DA leader Helen Zille likely would not have come out alive if she had dared venture into their predicament, and she knew as much. At that time Mamphela Ramphele was starting out as a political activist, but for all her past credentials, she would have been unlikely to survive in their midst either. The miners in Wonderkop represented a raw side of reality and though their anger had been simmering for quite a few years, the lid did not begin to lift until 2012 as they begin to rise up against the country's crude economic statistics. When they did, they were a formidable force who could not be easily talked down.

But how precarious has it become when a president of a country appears so far removed from his own people that he cannot stand in front of them and address them, in this case to extend his sympathies to them? Worse still, how slippery is the slope when the authorities feel the need to draft in the police to forcefully end a labour dispute? I recall Niel Barnard, the former spy chief from the apartheid era, once telling me that his regime knew it had finally lost control when parts of the country could only be governed by the presence of armoured police vehicles, and now, in August 2012, democratic South Africa appeared to be faring no better.

At that time little had been heard of Malema, who had been expelled from the ANC six months earlier after a gruelling disciplinary process that had started the previous August. First

the party decided to suspend him for a period of five years, but he challenged that decision. However, on appeal the party chose to expel him, feeling he had done little other than belittle the ANC while he was awaiting for his appeal to be heard. Still not satisfied, Malema chose to appeal the expulsion, even though by then he was showing nothing but disdain for the party he had once said he would die a member of. The decision to expel him was upheld and he was eventually removed from the ANC register on 25 April.

Throughout his years of political celebrity, Malema's brushes with the authorities had become legendary. In the first few months of 2010 he was convicted of hate speech by the Equality Court when he suggested Zuma's rape accuser enjoyed her ordeal because 'those who had a nice time will wait until the sun comes out, request breakfast and ask for taxi money', as he alleged she had done.

He was found guilty of hate speech in 2011 for resurrecting the song 'Shoot the Boer', which was loaded with racial sensitivities and tensions. That November he was suspended from the ANC and the following February he was expelled. Later that year, while he was acclimatising to the icy political wilderness, he was charged with fraud, money-laundering and racketeering. He was hounded by SARS for tax evasion, which had escalated to a whopping R18 million when he proposed to settle the bill in 2014, by which time he had already been provisionally sequestrated anyway. The Public Protector had investigated him twice, while a number of forensic investigating firms are still probing his involvement in the collapse of the Limpopo fiscus. Malema was a notorious chancer.

As his one-time critic turned political groupie Andile Mngxitama once wrote about him: 'Behind every great fortune there is a great crime'.

One of Malema's greatest strengths, however, is his ability to spot an opportunity. With his reputation still in tatters he made his way to Marikana and paraded straight into the political space that Zuma had unwittingly created for him. It was the Saturday after the massacre and with two microphones in his left hand, he stood atop a box speaker, decked out in a blue and red tracksuit, and began to trot out his old war words, telling the thousands of miners who had gathered to hear him that they must fight to their death for their economic freedom, irrespective of what the authorities might say or do.

'From today, when asked "Who is your president?", you must say, "I don't have a president",' he urged them, before encouraging them to push for the R12 500 they had benchmarked as a decent living wage and to stop at nothing until they got it.

Zuma must have been cringing to watch Malema steal his thunder in the manner he did, but he had only himself to blame. Expelling a force like Malema from the ANC was about as foolish as the decision to send the police in to Wonderkop.

Malema didn't a care a whit for what Zuma thought that day, however. As he watched the thousands of men who were hanging on to his every word, he knew he had found his new political home. He was preaching to a critical section of the country's underclass and that was the day he decided to become their leader.

Chapter 13

A harbinger of a new fate

When you are thirty-two, politically homeless, allegedly bankrupt and with a string of corruption and fraud charges crowding out your shadow, your next chapter is sure to be radical. Julius Malema's certainly was. Hence when the founders of the Economic Freedom Fighters (EFFs) began to plot their future, they cast their net as wide as it would fetch by starting a radical people's movement that would become the political home of the country's large and sprawling underclass, which by then accounted for around thirty million or so angry men and women.

The EFFs were the new revolutionaries and they underpinned their founding manifesto with socialist theory and peppered it with pledges to the thinking of Karl Marx and Vladimir Lenin, as well as Frantz Fanon. They dipped into a back catalogue of socialist messages and pulled out quotes from the likes of Amílcar Cabral and the late Burkina Faso hero Thomas Sankara. Che Guevara also featured and the late Hugo Chávez. They aspired to deliver on the goals of Black Consciousness and described themselves as anti-imperialists, anti-capitalists and generally anti-white and all things pale (usually filed under the heading of racist nationalism).

All well and good if you are going to be genuine about it, but if what you are really doing is founding a political party on the personal values of a womb-to-tomb dictator like Malema and allowing people of the ilk of Floyd Shivambu to become the enabler of your psychosis, then you are doomed. I suspect the EFF already is.

Though the EFF was officially launched in October 2013, the aggressive push for economic freedom began many years earlier, and harks back to Malema's Youth League days when he began to call for the nationalisation of the country's mines. Nationalisation is, many agree, a bad idea and something that has recorded only a few successes anywhere in the world, but for Malema it provided the means to deliver on the second phase of the so-called National Democratic Revolution (NDR): economic freedom.

The NDR is something the ANC ascribes to, but often in the way it says it also believes in the socialist spirit of the Freedom Charter, which boils down to little more than an occasional polite salute. Since it came to power in 1994, the former liberation movement has walked a very fine line in laying the foundations for the democracy, and it is by sheer luck rather than clever strategy that it managed to keep the nationalisation debate muffled for as long as it did.

Then along came Malema, who extinguished that relatively brief candle of opportunity when he sounded that clarion call for resource nationalism, which was first made in the winter of 2009, by which time his radicalism as the new League president had already captured the minds of the public through a very attentive media. Whenever Malema called a press conference, he was guaranteed significant coverage and his demands for a

majority share of the country's trillion-dollar mines to be placed in the hands of the state were widely noted that June. These were also the early days of the Zuma presidency, when people were still uncertain about which direction the country was headed under the so-called Polokwane pirates, and considering Malema was regarded as one of Zuma's power brokers, his movements were very carefully monitored at that time.

Though he spoke in the name of the Youth League when he made that initial call for nationalisation, in the months and years that followed he came to own the debate as if it were him alone taking on big capital and it was near impossible to hear mention of nationalisation without a direct reference to Malema.

Of course he also quite fancied himself in the light that it cast him because now that the horse had bolted, the prospect of resource nationalism stayed firmly at the centre of the national agenda over the course of the next four years, and with it Malema became a figure of significant concern for both local and international investors for whom the prospect of enhanced state control of the private sector was now suddenly quite real. Granted, the publicity he was generating was, in the main, quite negative, but he was becoming internationally renowned on the back of it. And it was at the height of that debate that he took to calling himself the commander-in-chief of economic freedom, a title he would later insist on adopting when he founded the EFF.

The nationalisation debate refused to go away and by the time 2010 came round, when the ANC held its national general council – that 'halfway checkpoint' between their five-yearly national conferences – the only way the ruling party could keep the noisy transformation calls at bay was to commission a thorough analysis of nationalisation around the world, complete with best-case and worst-case scenarios. By then Irvin Jim, the

head of the National Union of Metalworkers of South Africa (NUMSA), the country's largest union, had nailed his colours to Malema's mast, not because he had any personal or political affiliation with the Youth League president, but because he firmly believed in a socialist South Africa and when the Youth League conducted its own nationalisation feasibility study, it was Jim who bankrolled it with NUMSA funds.

All this coincided with another critical event: the unfolding of the blue-collar workers' revolution, referred to elsewhere in this book, and what was becoming apparent, even as early as 2011, was the refusal of these workers to accept the kind of slave wages that had come to define their existence.

The consequences were naturally dire for the union federation COSATU, but more so for the ANC, Malema's political home. He was truly out of control by then and regardless of what measures the party leadership might take to have him tow the line, it was clear the young man had already stretched his political wings. When he was re-elected for a second term as ANC Youth League president in June of 2011, his victory speech was laden with threats to take the League into fighting territory, not only to challenge the power base of Zuma, but, more importantly, to become the vanguard of the working class, and to fill the gaping 'vacuum' he insisted the ruling party had created.

A couple of months later the ANC hardened its stance when it slapped him with another set of disciplinary charges and by all accounts it seemed to be less forgiving then than it had been a year earlier. But regardless of what the organisation might do to him this time round, it was never going to be more than a gash in his hide, and pride, because as the harbinger of the country's new fate, he was deep in the trenches of economic freedom fighting by then anyway.

While still hanging on to his Youth League platform during the eight months it took the ANC to expel him, he staged the economic freedom march, when he and thousands of youths walked the seventy or more kilometres from the Chamber of Mines in downtown Johannesburg to the Union Buildings in Pretoria, stopping off at the Johannesburg Stock Exchange in Sandton along the way and handing out their demands en route. They dubbed it the longest protest march in world history, though it must be noted that the portly rebel was forced to hitch a ride for most of it, only to be whisked away at the end of it on a chartered flight to Mauritius to attend the lavish wedding bash of property developer David Mabilu. Still, Malema and his peers insist that march will 'go down in history as part of the set of protest actions that propelled the coming revolution'.[2]

When that awful massacre happened in Marikana in August 2012, Malema was quick to mine the broader political opportunity it presented and he stepped right into the 'vacuum' he had warned of a year earlier. As he spoke to the miners that Saturday, he trotted out a lot of his old messages, clinging to his by now familiar 'economic freedom in our lifetime' pitch. All that was different that afternoon was his audience and he gave them a strong shot of revolutionary jargon, which appealed to them enormously in that very dark moment.

From the sidewalks of South African life he then began his slow return to public life, preaching to the underclass and the underprivileged in tones of his characteristic crankiness and cant, always with the air of a man well used to being heard. In that brief period after he parted ways with the ANC and before forming the EFF, men and women in informal settlements and townships had taken to repeating his words and talking openly about what 'Malema says' and the promises he was soon to deliver on. Social media was jam-packed with talk of

his appearances and his utterances cut straight to the heart of the disgruntlement of the poor. As always, he had a tremendous knack for saying the right thing at the right time.

In the early months of 2013 his followers, many of them from the ANC Youth League who had left in solidarity with him, began to test the appetite among the poor and the marginalised for a new political party. By all accounts, there was a ready following for the kind of politics they were proposing. The country was also leaderless at that time, despite Jacob Zuma's re-election as the president of the ruling party a few months earlier.

As an aside, some time around then, I recall Malema being interviewed on radio by a presenter who tried to get tough with him when he asked if Malema was not capable of changing his tune when it came to Zuma. Was he not possessed with the strength of character to see anything positive in his erstwhile ally?

'No, I have always said that Zuma is a great singer and dancer,' the quick-witted Malema intoned. 'And I believe he will go down in the ANC's history books as the best singing and dancing president the ANC has ever had.'

Various informal meetings and discussions were held around South Africa in the first half of 2013 as the EFF's foundations were being laid and finally, on 11 June, at a meeting in the Protea Wanderers Hotel in Johannesburg, a decision was taken to start a new party that would deliver on the following key areas, which have become known within the party as their guiding 'seven pillars':

- Expropriation of South Africa's land without compensation for equal distribution.
- Nationalisation of mines, banks and other strategic sectors of the economy.
- Building of state and government capacity, which would lead to the eradication of tenders.

- Free quality education, healthcare, housing and sanitation.
- Industrial development that would create sustainable employment (with decent minimum living wages).
- Development of the African economy and an earnest push to move from reconciliation to justice throughout the continent.
- An open, accountable and corruption-free government and society without fear of victimisation by state agencies.

The message that emanated from that June meeting, and which was distributed widely on social media platforms, was essentially the following: if the seven pillars appeal to you, and if you think they will help shape the kind of future that you want to be a part of, then let's start a political party.

'It is important to highlight that this call genuinely sought guidance from the people [as to whether or not we should start an organisation],' Malema later said in an address to the nascent party. 'We believe that political organisations ought to be initiated by the people.'

'The name of Economic Freedom Fighters was decided spontaneously by the people, who responded that there should be an independent political formation, and as people who were at the forefront of these discussions, we embraced the name.'[3]

A second meeting followed on 10 July at the 17 Shaft conference centre in Johannesburg (ironically where Malema had attempted to bully his way into the presidency of COSAS more than a decade earlier) where core policy issues were discussed, but it was only later that month, on 26 July, that a formal decision was taken to launch a new party during a national assembly that took place at Uncle Tom's Hall in Orlando West, Soweto. That is the official birthdate of the EFF.

By then the red berets had become the signature caps of the new revolutionaries. Ahead of their first press conference, convened at Constitution Hill the day following the July policy meeting, Malema had asked Shivambu to get him a red beret. He had become used to wearing black berets for appropriately militant occasions throughout his political career, having donned his first one as early as 1990 when he was pint-sized and beginning to acquaint himself with the ANC. In his dying years in the Youth League, he reached for his black beret at each rebellious turn as he underwent his metamorphosis from an African nationalist. The cap was resurrected again for the 'economic freedom' march in 2011. But this was 2013 and he was now a committed socialist and desperately wanted a red one. Shivambu surprised him when he pitched up at the press conference with a cap for each of the 'commissars' present.

Those caps became the most ingenious branding gimmick, and also a clever fundraising tool during the election campaign that was ahead of them. But more of that later.

Featured in the family portrait that day at Constitution Hill were the colourful schleb Kenny Kunene, former MK veteran Mpho Ramakatsa, the self-believing 'super-black' Andile Mngxitama, the former *Generations* actor Fana Mokoena, Shivambu and twenty or so others, whom Malema introduced as the face of the new fight.

They were in full battle mode from those very early days and they structured the new organisation accordingly. They did not want to resort to the more pedestrian structures of 'executive committees' or titles such as 'president' or 'chairperson', simply because they were calling for a revolution that demanded a radical and militant approach. They styled the party on communist- and socialist-type structures, and the end product was an EFF headed by a commander-in-chief, a second layer of authority known

as the National Central Command Team (which included Julius Malema as Commander-in-Chief and Mpho Ramakatsa as National Coordinator, along with Floyd Shivambu, Kenny Kunene, Mbuyiseni Ndlozi, Sam Tshabalala, Fana Mokoena, Leigh-Ann Mathys, Pabane Moteka, Hlayiseka Chawane, Sipho Mbatha, Mandisa Makesini, Hlengiwe Hlophe and Andile Mngxitama), and beneath that again a horde of commissars responsible for various areas of political instruction and policy formation and organisation. They were the new regime-in-waiting.

The words of *The Eighteenth Brumaire of Louis Bonaparte* by Karl Marx come to mind:

> Men make their own history, but they do not make it as they please … The tradition of all dead generations weighs like a nightmare on the brains of the living. And just as they seem to be occupied with revolutionizing themselves and things, creating something that did not exist before, precisely in such epochs of revolutionary crisis they anxiously conjure up the spirits of the past to their service, borrowing from them names, battle slogans, and costumes in order to present this new scene in world history in time-honored disguise and borrowed language.[4]

Naturally, Malema's red army was lampooned to begin with. Even when they returned to Marikana for their official launch on 13 October of that year, to the spot where he had sealed his political fate in the wake of the massacre of the miners a year earlier, few believed his revolutionary politics would gain popular traction. But then again, the prospect of the popular will becoming self-destructive in South Africa had always been underestimated.

Chapter 14

Populism and power

Like not a few populists before him, Julius Malema turned his totemic charm up full blast in the months that followed the launch of the EFF and by the time 2013 began to ebb into 2014, he was the new sun in South Africa's universe. He and his EFFers began to descend on every grit-strewn backwater and informal settlement in the country, spreading their socialist message wide now that the campaign for the May elections was in full swing.

Of South Africa's 30 or so million eligible voters, only 17 million had partaken in the previous elections, the rest of them choosing to drift outside the system of a country that was now on its way to becoming another ordinary African story, leaving an ample and available market for the new socialists to trade in.

Malema had referred to this when he launched the EFF the previous year, when he asked, rhetorically, 'Where are the others? We will talk to them. There is going to be action everywhere. We will be among our people.'

Sure enough, they were. 'Like the Holy Spirit', as he said of himself while defending his use of expensive helicopters to criss-cross the country at the height of the campaign. With adamantine strength, he gave one rafter-raising speech after another to 'his people', as he arrogantly referred to the black poor, promising them a bounty of social wealth in return for their votes.

According to the party's election manifesto, the social grants would immediately double in value for all sixteen million recipients in a welfare system that was already setting the state back more than R122 billion a year in its current form. The EFF promised to create 'millions' of jobs and provide free houses, as well as heavily subsidised electricity for their occupants. The intake of black students to universities would also double, 'with mechanisms to ensure high pass rates to be put in place to ensure their success'. The minimum wage would rise to R4 500, and for mineworkers would stretch to R12 500, while civil servants would see their pay cheques increase significantly.

To fund the socialist state, the EFF said it would take control of all land without compensating its owners, nationalise all the mines, the private banks and the strategic sectors of the economy, and then channel all the money into a state-owned bank that would in turn dole out the dues to 'our people'. The party wanted to start a state-owned construction company that would be responsible for building all houses, structures and roads. There would be a state-owned cement company to supply their needs, a state-owned pharmaceutical company, and a state-owned food-stocking company 'to regulate prices of basic foodstuffs and guarantee food security for all'.

A radical overhaul of policy such as the EFF was offering was conveying the very profound message that henceforth we look after ourselves, the black poor, regardless of what the international investment community might do or say. Of course it was utopian, but for the millions of desperate South Africans who were searching for a (black) alternative, the EFF was presenting the concept of 'economic freedom' in ways that no other party would dare to. Whether its means to achieve it were plausible or not was almost irrelevant; the fact that it was

offering the poor the possibility to think about an alternative to twenty years of hardship was novel. The party was presenting them with an imagined escape route to poverty and, in so doing, dismantling the monopoly the ANC held over them.

Malema's timing was impeccable as the frustration of the black poor was palpable, evident not only by the rolling service delivery protests countrywide, but also the labour unrest that had been spreading across the economy since 2011.

It was 'a struggle between the past and the future', as Malema described it, a tug at the interregnum that is referred to elsewhere in this book.

For a very young party with little or no financial backing,[5] the EFF was clever in the way it approached that campaign. There were a few silent donors, many of them drawn from the community of frustrated small- and medium-sized business owners, but their contributions were relatively minor. There were others who contributed 'in kind', such as the owner of the helicopter that ferried Malema around, but one of the EFF's most clever drivers of revenue was the formidable red beret, an accidental gimmick in the party's early days. The caps were branded with the EFF's logo and lettering and sold at R80 a piece, but only in bulk, in quantities of one hundred and upward, and they were flogged through party headquarters in Braamfontein, in downtown Johannesburg, or through the coordinators and convenors that were appointed to each of the nine provinces. Some of the provincial heads resold them at a higher cost and pumped the added revenue back into their respective provincial campaigns or into the national coffers.

The berets were an ingenious marketing tool and another weapon in Malema's arsenal, all of it part of his political theatre. To wear one of those caps was to convey the kind of resistance

and revolutionary zeal that undergirded the EFF. You were one of the new commandos, pounding the tarmac to the beat of Malema's militant demands, and those red caps became a 'must-have' fashion accessory for the 2014 elections. And you have to admit, they made for an affecting picture.

After the berets, the bright red workers' overalls made their debut, another item of branded apparel intended to convey solidarity with the struggle of the working classes, though they were nowhere near as successful as the revolutionary red caps. On the pot-bellied Malema, who had taken to wearing red hard hats when he didn't have a red beret sitting on his shiny pate, the ill-fitting 'onesie' looked ridiculous, but he wore it unashamedly, even to the national assembly, at one stage completing his outfit with a pair of designer slip-on shoes.

'If you were a Teletubby, even Tinky Winky would suggest you go on a diet,' humorist Ben Trovato bitched at Malema.

Yet for the party's election poster, Malema posed in a neat, Western-style suit and crisp shirt and tie, confusing his critics and constituents alike. What was this if not socio-political cross-dressing? Why he deemed it necessary to break from the working-man's attire is beyond me, but what baffles me even more is why he opted for those red overalls as his political 'uniform' to begin with when the EFF's core target group were the jobless, the underclass, who are infinitely greater in number than the working class (who, incidentally, are actually fewer in number than those holding private health insurance, which gives you a sense of the crisis facing the country when the income tax base is so low). Granted, it was all about that 'affecting photo', but who were they fooling when they had to resort to costumes and 'dressing up' to convince their constituents, if not themselves, that they were one of them?

What was also glaring was the scant support Malema received from his erstwhile friends and allies in the ANC, none of whom appeared willing to go slumming with him in his new socialist venture. Many of them had vanished like breath off a razor blade as soon as he was expelled and he failed to attract any really big names into the EFF's ranks. With the exception of Floyd Shivambu, the respected Mpho Ramakatsa, and colourful figures such as Kenny Kunene and Dali Mpofu, the rest were by and large relatively unknown men and women from the ANC Youth League.

Malema's friendship with Fikile Mbalula, his one-time partner in political crime, was long gone. The pair is no longer even on speaking terms. His ties to Tokyo Sexwale, a one-time benefactor, were severed. Even Winnie Madikizela-Mandela, one of his biggest supporters, if not his mentor, turned down his socialist advances.

Shortly after he joined the EFF, Mpofu visited Madikizela-Mandela at her Soweto home, at Malema's behest, to see if they could lure her over. If she dallied briefly with the idea, she never took the matter further and didn't return Malema's calls when he tried phoning her, yet she openly supported him and the EFF. I interviewed her during the last few months of 2013, not about the EFF but about the now late Madiba, and she was unwavering in her support for Malema and was quick to introduce him into the conversation. I suspect that deep down, and on an ideological level, she would have felt more at home with Malema's new revolutionary ideals than with the conservative party she belonged to, but she was in her late seventies by then and the ANC was etched deeply into her DNA.

Malema also tried to form alliances with various structures and individuals to enhance his vote share but there were only

a few of his targets who would trust him enough to align with him. The troubled COSATU chief Zwelinzima Vavi was high on Malema's list, but he refused to budge. NUMSA was threatening to start its own political party but its leadership was not willing to entertain an EFF coalition of any description. The small and relatively young Workers and Socialists Party was offered two places on the EFF's Central Command Team, but they refused to accept its leader (a white woman), on the basis that she was pale-skinned and also a foreigner.

The hugely popular Association of Mineworkers and Construction Union (AMCU) was and remains a key target for Malema because it is regarded as the only genuinely pro-worker union by the blue-collar workforce. However, since its inception, AMCU has been adamant not to align with any political party, which has become one of its key selling points, so Malema was forced to lobby its members informally instead and by the time the May elections were held, the vast majority of AMCU members were EFF sympathisers and voters. It presents an interesting dynamic as Malema is evidently intent on capturing AMCU, which is not without its own internal tensions, and the end result can only be disastrous.

Hence the EFF was forced to face into the 2014 elections alone, but the party performed remarkably well and stunned its critics when it won more than a million votes. Though that translated to only 6.35 per cent of the vote share, the party had polled third after the ruling ANC and the official opposition party, the DA, and won twenty-five seats in the national parliament. The EFF also become the official opposition party in Malema's home province of Limpopo, and in the coveted province of Gauteng it won more than 11 per cent of the local vote.

South Africa's political system, until then heavily defined by a conservative black-dominated party (the ANC) and

a conservative white-dominated party (the DA), was now reconfigured with the arrival of the black-dominated socialist EFF. Though it would do little to deracialise the country's politics, it was about to reanimate the landscape by taking the public discourse outside the tired established framework in which it had operated for the past twenty years.

On 21 May Malema and twenty-four of his EFF members were sworn into parliament and they formed a red bloc of resistance in the opposition benches in their bright-coloured apparel. The men wore the 'onesies', by then a familiar sight, and the women wore the traditional outfits of the 'home help' and, of course, it was the EFF theatrics on the floor of the national assembly that captured the minds of the public throughout that day.

Certainly it was novel, if not a tad humorous to begin with, to see sitting MPs dressing up in this way, but there was a sense that the fun and games would begin to bore before too long. The EFF had an enormous opportunity to shake up the conservative parliament through rigorous and radical debate about key policy issues and if there was any party possessed with the skill and the wit to do it, it was them. It may surprise many to know that several of the EFF's MPs hold university degrees, three of them hold a Master's, while one is a chapter away from completing his Doctorate at Wits University and another is a medical doctor. At least two of them hold post-matric qualifications and a couple of them, if not more, have attended the Thabo Mbeki African Leadership Institute.[6] Yet there is already a sense that the EFFers will foolishly spend more time inveighing against the system of parliament with one brazen stunt after another, rather than fighting the bigger system they were elected to challenge.

167

Consider Malema's maiden speech halfway through June and his withering remark about the ANC's involvement in the Marikana massacre, which had him thrown out of parliament when he frigidly refused to withdraw it. It was a memorable moment, but there is perhaps not another word of that speech that anyone can meaningfully recall or contextualise. The abiding image is of him untying his tongue and being booted out of the house with his radical entourage in tow. It was soon followed by the fiasco in the Gauteng and Eastern Cape provincial legislatures where EFF members were asked to leave because of the party attire. Malema immediately responded with a threat 'to make Gauteng ungovernable', but how many times have we heard those ranting words before?

Though it is perhaps early days, Malema and his party may be underestimating the anger and desperation of the constituency they represent, who will see through the theatrics before long. When I visited Marikana late in 2013 to gauge the support for the EFF, it was evident that Malema had laid his foundations well, but it was abundantly clear that those who had already decided to support him were desperately seeking results, and in 'quick time'. That was less than six months ahead of the vote, but what was fascinating was the extent to which people talked more about the next generation than the next elections. In the main, they were looking towards union leaders to deliver on the kind of jobs that would help to create a future for them and their families rather than political leaders who they believed had failed them since 1994. If Malema could give them what they were looking for, they were willing to give him a chance, but if not, they are no longer prepared to hang about in their misery waiting.

This phenomenon of pinning hopes on unions rather than political parties is a global one and is well documented in *The*

Coming Jobs War, a book published by the United States polling firm Gallup. It explains the enormous pressures that are now placed on trade union movements, but more importantly warns against the dangers of filling people with false hopes, which is precisely what the populist EFF appears to be doing. Even within its own ranks, members are becoming frustrated at what they see as a departure from their own ideals and commitments. Before its launch, the EFF's would-be founders aligned with the September National Imbizo (SNI), a platform started by Andile Mngxitama some years back, which is inspired by Black Consciousness and abides by what it calls the 'Sankara Oath'.

The name is in reference to the guiding principles of Thomas Sankara, the late Marxist revolutionary who came to power on the back of a military coup in the former French colony of Upper Volta in 1983. He renamed the country Burkina Faso, meaning 'the land of upright [or incorruptible] people', and attempted to roll out an enormously ambitious people-centred social and economic reform plan. Though Sankara's politics was controversial and heavily authoritarian, by the time he was assassinated in 1987 he was a hero of the African poor and known among them as the continent's Che Guevara.

When the SNI drafted the Sankara Oath, it was to ensure that in the event that it ever went into government, the members would, as public representatives, avail themselves of all public services on offer. When the EFF decided to adopt the oath in 2013, it was also with the pledge 'that public representatives should use public services', based on Sankara's ethos which 'meant that he lived an ordinary life and did not fall into the temptations and luxuries that often come with the occupation of public office. The Sankara values are admirable and something which the EFF Founding Manifesto encapsulates.'[7]

Any attempt to liken Malema to Sankara is, of course, laughable. It was because of Malema that the term 'tenderpreneur' was introduced into the South African lexicon in 2009, and it is argued that it is because of his ties to a number of controversial multimillion-rand tenders that he is now fighting a string of corruption, fraud and money-laundering charges in the courts. To that add Malema's insistence a few days after he was sworn into parliament that he would continue sending his son, Ratanang, to an elite private school in place of the public schools his party has pledged to support.

That last statement rattled his party base enormously, but there was little they could do about it as Malema is not challenged in the EFF, not even by his Central Command, the highest-ranking leadership team. It was for this reason, among others, that Kenny Kunene resigned from the party not long after it was launched in 2013. Not that Kunene has been a poster boy for moral regeneration, but it was the sense of suffocation that was penetrating the EFF that bothered him.

Malema is an excellent politician and he is arguably one of the most skilled in the country. He knows what to do, what to say and where to say it. And all credit to him for identifying the opportunity that existed in the South African spectrum and for articulating the sense that if poverty is not radically addressed in the coming years, South Africa is facing a very grim future. But Malema is a man who is more committed to himself than to the ideals of socialism and it would seem the culture that is unfolding now in the EFF is but another version of the crisis he left behind in the Youth League.

Chapter 15

It's complicated

Looking back, it is almost as if Julius Malema appeared out of nowhere around the middle of 2008. One day he wasn't there, and the next there he was, ploughing the socio-political landscape like an unguided missile, with little or no let-up ever since.

It marked an extraordinary turn of events. For years, the world had admired the iconic stature of the late Nelson Mandela, the peaceful and noble product of a bitter struggle that lasted for more than forty years and put an end to racial injustice that had lingered for centuries. Then along came Malema, the product of one hundred years of struggle politics. South Africans took a sharp intake of breath.

In his days as a budding ANC strongman, Malema never held public office and his most senior ranking was only the head of the ruling party's youth wing, and yet he was arguably the most prominent and talked about of all of the post-1994 cadres. It was not simply his aggressive style of politics that helped market his radical brand but the fact that he was something of an oddity, a man who crossed several social boundaries in a country defined by stark separations. He belonged to the political elite, but could also call himself one of the masses. He was a representative of the youth, yet was leading his seniors by the nose. He was ridiculed

for his lack of formal education, though he had pulled off one of the most extraordinary political coups of all time by securing his place in the front line in the manner that he did. He had a knack for living life close to the edge yet could still maintain his political footing, if not among the ANC's leadership then for sure among his significant following.

The liberal and conservative sections of South African society were mesmerised by him, though not necessarily enamoured with him. They followed his every move, though they didn't always get him. In his days in the ANC Youth League, they attached to him the 'single story' of which Chimamanda Ngozi Adichie talks, the narrative that unfolds through the aperture of a narrow lens, but that only narrowed their understanding of him. He was a product of his past, tangled and tempered with the socio-economic conditions of today, but they were a product of a very different past.

Malema's rise to prominence, first in the ANC Youth League and later in the EFF, flagged an even bigger disconnect. In the interregnum that has engulfed the country, there is no longer only one South Africa but several, each one trying to make sense of the other. Each one is real, each one a product of various pasts and presents. Yet each one is also tangled up in the process of trying to forge an identity somewhere between the old and the new.

And that's what makes any real understanding of Malema difficult. His prominence in political life comes at a critical time, when many South Africans are beginning to settle into the new South Africa while others are beginning to rise up at the prospect of being left behind. He lives in a country that is underpinned by a sophisticated first-world economy yet is bogged down by the harsh realities of the third world. Look no further than

the mining belt where he plies his trade on a daily basis. In the early years following 1994 the very same discomforts existed but society chose to give the ANC the benefit of the doubt, if not a very comfortable period of time to find its footing, on the back of the promise that it would eventually deliver on the goals of the transition. However, all that changed with the eruption of South Africa's Arab Spring, manifested through the ongoing labour unrest, in the thick of which was Malema putting words on it all in treacherous and menacing tones.

It's complicated. Very, very complicated. Not Malema, but the environment he inhabits and the period of time in which he lives.

To repeat the words of Antonio Gramsci: 'The old is dying, and the new cannot be born; in this interregnum there arises a great diversity of morbid symptoms.'

It is not my suggestion that Malema is such a morbid symptom, but instead a product of poverty, politics, power and a racial past of which he won't let go. He, and all that he stands for, is complex. Yet the likes of him should come as no surprise in a society that is not only still divided along racial lines but is also teetering on a lethal mix of all those unfulfilled promises from the transition, gross inequality in socio-economic terms, and a weak ANC that rules on a majority vote and lives off the possibilities of politics.

Malema is not alone. There are countless Malemas out there, harbouring hurts, hopes and grand ambitions. When Sarah Malema described her grandson's upbringing, she talked of a young boy reared in morbid misery and poverty; and as she did, she told the story of most South African youth then and now. She told the story of survival, one that is not confined to South Africa but which is a worldwide phenomenon.

'It's about eating or being eaten,' says anthropologist Rehana Vally. 'It's about beating or being beaten. It's about survival. It's

human.' As Malema grew up, entered his teens and then matured into manhood, that sense of survival stayed with him, because in him is a fighter who never ceases to fight. There are few like him with such a 'fuck you' attitude to life, largely white life, and each time he opens his mouth to talk, he taps into the psychosocial features of many South Africans.

'People really desperately want to show a finger to all the white symbols and all that comes with them. And Malema does it on their behalf,' says author and social commentator Max du Preez. 'And they sit there and they enjoy it in their hearts. Here's a young man, son of a domestic worker, comes from a poor township, and he goes on national television and says "fuck you" to white people. They want to say it. But they can't. And they love him because he does. And he got that.'

What Malema also gets is the anger that is etched into the South African psyche. He gets the negrophobia and the self-hatred because they are psychological features that he too harbours.

The self-hatred comes from knowing you are 'hated, despised, detested, not by the neighbour across the street ... but by an entire race', as Frantz Fanon put it more than half a century ago when he was explaining the South African phenomenon in *Black Skin, White Masks*.[8] That must have been a fairly powerful feeling on the part of those whites who forced themselves to despise all blacks the way in which they did, not because they had committed some awful crime or atrocity, but simply because they were black, even though the so-called natives were the majority living on home turf. At the time that Fanon was writing, in 1952, South Africa was 'a boiler into which 13 million blacks were clubbed and penned in by two-and-a-half million whites ... in a racist structure'.[9] Not all of those whites would have harboured

such illogical racism, but those who did, and they were the vast majority, strongly believed that each individual black was unworthy, insubordinate, wicked and living on the wrong side of life. They held those views so strongly that they legislated against the so-called native. And they sustained that hatred for decades.

As powerful as those feelings must have been, they would have been no match for the feelings of anger, shame and humiliation they instilled in each black individual, a humiliation that stemmed from the superiority complex which whites endowed upon themselves, which in itself is a necessary ritual in the crude act of racism, as necessary as the feeling of inferiority which blacks were and sometimes still are forced to inculcate and accept.

'And it has never occurred to a single black to consider himself superior to a member of the white minority,' Fanon argued fifty years ago.[10]

Why didn't they? Perhaps because a life lived in humiliation often weakens a person and can force him or her to doubt and even hate him- or herself. And those who hate themselves tend to be very angry and insecure individuals. That anger will always have to find an outlet, which Malema usually finds today in white society when he regularly rails against what he calls 'white tendencies'.

'I am not racist,' he says in defence. 'When I talk about "white tendencies" I am talking about anything that seeks to maintain white supremacy. That is what I cannot support.'

I do believe Malema when he says he is not racist. I don't believe it is racism per se that makes his blood boil, but instead the lack of transformation he sees around him and the attitude by many sections of white society that reminds him that once

he was inferior. And that this attitude still continues to this day is what gets him on his hind legs. I firmly believe that much is genuine.

As suggested earlier, Malema looks at life as a man with an opponent. In his understanding of life there is always an enemy. As he harks back to the 1940s and the way in which the ANCYL marched in a militant manner against the white-led regime, he knows that to do so today requires an enemy. And he has mentally assembled the whites into his firing line. Fine though the line is between seeing the whites as the enemy and being racist, I still lean towards the former in his case.

But rather than turn around the lack of transformation, he tries to fight it and in doing that he lays bare unwanted tensions all over the country. The EFF's proposals to grab land, resources and key sectors of the economy are hardly a solution to the current predicament. South Africa would end up with a civil war on its hands if Malema were to win the kind of power he is hankering after because it is always based on race.

Yet it is not Malema but his mother and his grandmother and her mother before her who were born and bred in a country that was defined by racism. Malema was born thirteen years before apartheid came to an end and he grew up in the swing of the transition, at a time when opportunities existed for blacks as never before. By the time he reached his teens, the world was his oyster. When he turned eighteen, he had the right to vote, unlike his elders before him. The party he chose to be affiliated with was no longer outlawed. He grew up in an era that was defined by democracy and he could have been anything or done anything with his life. Yet he developed a life-size chip on his shoulder and an angry outlook on certain aspects of life.

His anger was nurtured in the society that bred him, a society that is grounded in victimisation and one that is still deeply

fractured and segregated with no common or shared identity in any lasting or meaningful sense.

South Africa showed the world just how angry it could be in the winter of 2008, ironically the same time that Malema became the president of the ANC Youth League, when more than sixty people were brutally killed in a ghastly slaughter of so-called xenophobia. Yet two years later the country threw its arms open to the world in a display of xenophilia when it staged a successful and enjoyable FIFA World Cup. But the morning after the football final was played, scenes of xenophobia were recorded in Cape Town and tensions erupted elsewhere around the country.

How can a society produce such extreme behaviour in so short a period of time? Or is xenophobia perhaps a mistaken term for something more awful at play in South African society? Is negrophobia, rather than xenophobia, not a more apt term to describe the hatred that is often unleashed on fellow black Africans by black South Africans?

Negrophobia is not the monopoly of blacks, Achille Mbembe points out.

'If we think of negrophobia as the fear and hatred of other black Africans, then all South Africans share those feelings, black and white.

'And there is an "entanglement" of colours in South Africa, which is what gives Malema's person a different hue. He is the product of the dark undercurrents of South African history, across the colour lines and beyond them. There is no black history in South Africa that doesn't involve whiteness. The history is an entanglement of colour lines,' Mbembe says. His reasoning follows this thread: 'Like negrophobia, racism is not the monopoly of whites, just as self-hatred is not the monopoly of blacks. Whites hate themselves for not having been able to

establish a dominion like Canada, New Zealand or Australia. They consider themselves failures in relation to those other historical contexts.'

Blacks hate themselves because for centuries they were unable to withstand white oppression.

The same logic applies to racism, 'which is premised fundamentally on some unresolved conflict with oneself and is then projected onto some other who is stigmatised, especially when you have the power to do so,' Mbembe adds.

Malema has exhibited as much of this kind of behaviour as many white men have before him. The verbal abuse he hurled at the journalist who gave him some lip during a press conference at the ANC headquarters, what Malema later referred to as 'my own house', was a case in point. The EFF's constant threat to wage a war against white society, the entire premise upon which the party rests, is another example of this. There will undoubtedly be many more until such time as he and society manage to settle the score with their past.

'So I would argue that Malema is an enunciation of the entanglement of black and white in South African life,' says Mbembe.

Malema is also a vehicle for the resentment that is felt towards the perceived cosmetic agreement or settlement of 1994. That the current order was not established by a classic revolution galls the likes of Malema.

'I wasn't around during the negotiations, but I'm here now ... We are leading now. We are running this country,' he told me once: words that are repeated elsewhere in this book and which speak volumes about Malema's outlook on life.

It is this 'fighting' kind of language that, in Mbembe's view, fuels a kind of 'lumpen radicalism' with which Malema has come

to be associated and which is 'nurtured by illiteracy, poverty and a very short-sighted radicalism'.

What partly fuelled that radicalism were the failures of the 1995 Truth and Reconciliation Commission (TRC), which was set up to try to help South African society disentangle the knots in its make-up and start to weave a social life afresh, though it never had a mandate to solve the South African issue. It was an attempt to bring people back to life, back from 'the narrow gate of the sepulchre where centuries of racism had forced them to reside', as Mbembe once put it.

But as Gillian Slovo, the daughter of the late and respected communist leader Joe Slovo, pointed out a few years ago in a piece she wrote for the online publication *Open Society* – comments which she says she still stands by – the TRC was born out of a compromise, from an agreement between the ANC and the National Party that none of the members of the apartheid regime, nor those who acted on its behalf, would be brought to book. Though the ANC did not want to cede the blanket amnesty which the National Party sought, it allowed for individual amnesties based on disclosure of crimes in the public court of the TRC.

In that regard, the TRC failed to bring the kinds of justice it promised.

'This was the nature of South Africa's agreement: the transfer of power without a previous settling of historic rights and wrongs,' Gillian Slovo argued. 'Out of a need to end bloodshed and to find a way forward, came political transformation of power without social transformation. As my father often used to put it: the day after the first democratic election (and thus after the inevitable change of government) South Africa would still be the same country as it had been the day before.'

That compromise was based on the belief that peace was more important than justice. Therefore sacrifice would replace

reconciliation, and the legacy of the transition, for many people, would amount to little more than a changing of the political guard.

The legacy of that compromise is multilayered and it drew out a band of political entrepreneurs, the likes of Malema, who now feed off the economically disenfranchised in order to create a place for themselves in the sun.

It also put a lid on the anger that had been nurtured through white oppression. The late Mandela was leading by example when he transcended the pain and suffering of his own walk to freedom and he expected tens of millions of South Africans to follow in his footsteps and do as he was doing.

But it was a short-sighted dream and the lid finally began to rise with the mounting tension that continued to bubble beneath it. The anger hadn't dissipated; it had simply continued to simmer until it eventually began to throw up the likes of Malema. By not facing up to racism, racism inadvertently became a legacy of the struggle rather than something the struggle had fought to put an end to, and in that way it encouraged a sense of victimhood, the other scourge that underwrites South African history and present-day society.

Victimhood started centuries ago when the Africans fell victim to the Boers in the 1600s. The Boers, following the Xhosas, later fell victim to the British after the Anglo-Boer War. The Africans became victims of both the Boers and the British, before and after apartheid in 1948. History turned the tables forty-six years later when Afrikaners and British South Africans perceived themselves as the new victims after the first democratic elections returned a black government. Today's society, with all its faults, has produced a large crop of Africans who feel they are victims of their own people because they have yet to find a place in the

new dispensation and, consequently, the new South Africa has created a body of victims who shuffle around in an increasingly fragile society weighed down by the ghosts of its past.

How does a society lay so many ghosts to rest? The businesswoman-turned-failed-politician Mamphela Ramphele tells a good tale in her book *Laying Ghosts to Rest* about the ghosts that haunted her childhood in the 1950s and how she tried to deal with them.

When Ramphele was growing up in the village of Kranspoort at the foot of the Soutpansberg Mountains in Limpopo, she developed a deep fear of darkness. Those were the days before electricity reached her part of the world and darkness permeated her life. What sparked her fear were not the dark nights themselves, but the ghosts that legend had led her to believe were haunting Kranspoort. They petrified Ramphele and there was only one person who could help her tame the ghosts, an old man by the name of Uncle Paulos. 'Uncle Paulos confronted each ghost by name. He would plead with the ghost to make peace with whatever unfinished business was troubling it, and find rest ... What Uncle Paulos did in each instance was to acknowledge the ghost by calling its name. This acknowledgement opened a channel of communication between the living and those in the afterlife. Unfinished business was acknowledged and peace was made.'[11]

But South Africa chose to turn its back on its unfinished business by refusing to face up to its past and name the ghosts that would haunt it into the future.

'Think back to Joe Slovo's words,' says Vally. 'South Africa a day later would still be the same South Africa as the day before. And for millions of South Africans today, this is still the old South Africa. They are not participating in the new South Africa.'

They are out on the margins, where they resided for forty years of apartheid and the centuries that went before it. Time eventually played its hand and the society that has emerged is the one we all inhabit: angry; self-hating; racially divided and racist; negrophobic; obscenely rich in some parts and desperately poor in others; often bleak and yet tragically hopeful; a mean and cruel society, yet one with a huge heart.

'And the brutality of the society we had during our past is still with us,' Vally continues. 'We see that brutality in the crime or the murders or in the domestic violence. The brutality is everywhere. But that brutality also gave rise to Malema.'

'Think about it,' she continues. 'What does it mean to be poor? What does it mean to survive when you are poor? You have to be brutal to get your morsel of food.'

Malema did what he had to when he was younger until he eventually pulled himself up by his socks, and various other means as it now transpires, to get to where he is today. In crude terms, he is a black man who has arrived, politically and financially, the former enhancing the latter and vice versa. But as he looks around him now, he sees opportunity staring him in the face. He sees a sea of poverty.

He sees more than fourteen million South Africans living on handouts from the state through one form of grant or another, people whom the state is on the one hand helping, but on the other hand telling 'you are not able to participate in this new South Africa, in this new economy'. In this new South Africa, if one is rich, one can consume. If one is poor, one simply cannot participate. Hence they are excluded. And the frightening fact is that more than half of all South Africans are now on the outside looking in. That's twenty-five or so million people. It's a staggering figure.

It is also an indirect admission on the part of government that it has failed to deliver on social justice. Mandela delivered the peace, but the social and economic justice, the real justice, has yet to come. The kind of justice that will allow people to live in well-built homes that have electricity and running water, and to access a decent health system and an education that will train them to take part in the market economy and live a life of dignity. All of this is still lacking.

It is a feature of South African life that existed long before Malema came onto our radars. It has its roots in the early days of the transition, as far back as 1994 when the ANC-led government hinged the enormous task of the transition on the Reconstruction and Development Programme (RDP), a national framework for social development that was initially defined by the country's trade unions, but later appropriated by the alliance that was about to govern the country. And with the blessing of Mandela, the country's first president, the RDP became the blueprint for transformation.

Despite the best intentions that inspired it, the plan was deeply flawed. It conceptualised the state as the sole arbiter of the transition, of the RDP, and in so doing it all but suffocated the voice of civil society. This in turn made people bystanders in their own lives, as Jay Naidoo, the minister with responsibility for the RDP, later admitted.

'What followed was a decade of state-led development,' he said, during which the political space also narrowed to such an extent that factionalism set in across the ANC and fear began to permeate society.

People became disaffected, not only because they were feeling excluded but also because they were being left behind. It began to dawn on them that if they were born in a shack in the new

South Africa, the chances were that they would depart to their graves from one as well. If they were born in the so-called second economy, they would be damned for life. They were the masses, a large underclass of society whose lives were marked by extreme poverty, and their ranks had swelled by the time Malema came to prominence in 2008 and took them under his wing.

By then they had taken to staging 'service delivery protests' to try to make themselves heard. Had Malema been listening, what would have echoed were their shrill cries appealing for someone to pull them out of the miserable hole of black, African life and integrate them into the mainstream of the new South Africa.

The first of these 'service delivery protests' was staged in 2004 in the small township of Intabazwe on the outskirts of Harrismith in the Free State and it rocked the country for the week or so that the fires flared. It was a new phenomenon for which no one had a name. Neither the protesters who staged the protest, the reporters who reported on it nor the commentators who tried to make sense of it initially knew what to call it. The locals were saying they had reached the end of their tether over the slow provision of basic services, such as water, roads and electricity, and had taken to pounding the tarmac. And so it was that the term 'service delivery protest' entered the South African lexicon.

In the following ten years, through to 2014 when the country celebrated two decades of freedom, hundreds and hundreds of such protests took place in different hot spots across South Africa. With the exception of one or two protests that get out of hand, by and large these street riots rarely manage to capture the public imagination any longer, even though they carry the voices of millions of South Africans who reside in pathetic states of deprivation, a message that any government ought not to ignore. Today, 'service delivery protests' have become a euphemism for ticking time bombs and serious social unrest.

The irony is that the vast majority of the protesters are ANC voters who have faithfully returned the ruling party to power four times since 1994, in the perpetual hope of that better life that was initially promised to them. However, as the most recent election results showed, their patience is beginning to wear thin.

One in every four South Africans is now living on state handouts. Of the country's youth it is estimated that every second one is jobless. More than six million people are living with the killer disease of HIV/AIDS. The mortality rate for children is worsening. Though school enrolment figures are improving, the percentage of teenagers completing Grade 12 is teetering around the 25 per cent mark. Crime continues to burden society with annual murder rates now five times the global average. The waiting list for a state house is so long that it is expected to take more than ten years to clear it. Between 2005 and 2006, when Malema was rising through his party's ranks, the poorest 20 per cent of South Africa's population lived off 1.4 per cent of available income. During that same period, 49 per cent of African households were earning less than R20 000 a year, according to Hein Marais in *South Africa Pushed to the Limit*.

These statistics have been trotted out numerous times before, but they are worth repeating for the sole purpose of hammering home a fundamental point: it is these unchanging social and economic indicators that partly helped to breathe political life into Julius Malema. And as he interpreted these statistics, he saw a powerful calling card on which he could begin to trade: the voiceless, the excluded, the angered, the furious.

Malema was cunning in his approach. He began to ask, 'Why are you poor?' And he formulated their answers for them: 'You are poor because too many white people are rich', a line he has clung to throughout his ANC days and into the EFF era.

Indirectly he is telling them, 'You are only good for your vote. And when you cast it, you get your grant in return.'

'Those who are on social grants are pushed further out on to the margins so that they are no longer the masters of their own destinies,' says Vally. 'And Malema knows that. And as he walks them by the hand, he is becoming the master of their destiny instead.'

'It has echoes of *Mein Kampf* to it all,' Vally continues. 'Germany of that era was exactly about economics. Poor Germans were told that the only reason they were poor was because Jewish people were controlling the economy.'

Hence when Malema came to prominence around 2008, he immediately began to talk the language of the disaffected, those who make up the largest and most important constituency in the country. He was already thinking of life after the Youth League. He knew it would be constituency politics that would determine his future in the way it had decided Mbeki's downfall and Zuma's comeback in 2007 (in which he had played a part). He knew it would be pointless for him to pin his ambitions on the youth vote alone, so he turned to the tens of millions who make up South Africa's so-called masses and presented himself as one of them, as a hapless victim of a dark era.

Of course he wasn't one of them. Malema's ship had come in many years earlier and he has not known a day of economic hardship ever since, despite his bankruptcy claims. But that did not stop him from talking up a compelling political line in favour of the disenchanted millions all around him, trading on waves of discontent that have helped carry him into the world of the overprivileged.

Malema began to choose his talking points carefully, finding his strongest form of expression in the failings of the promises

the ANC had made in 1994. He spotted the failures, crafted the solutions and promoted them on the back of the support of the millions of the masses who began to walk alongside him. He is most closely associated with the controversial debate around the nationalisation of the country's wealth, through which he plans to claw back ownership of the subsoil mineral assets that are valued in multiples of trillions of rand, along with key sectors of society. Had wealth in South Africa been more evenly distributed, or had the economy been more transformed, Malema would have found it difficult to broach the issue of state ownership of the mines or radical transformation of any kind. But the failure to do so gave him the kind of ammunition welcomed by any effective populist.

The government's aim was to have 25 per cent of the economy in black hands by 2017. But with statistics showing that the bulk of the economy is still skewed in favour of white ownership, and that white minority ownership of the country's strategic resources is increasing rather than decreasing, a situation was created that was begging for an overhaul, one which Malema chose to address with his radical call for nationalisation while still the head of the ANC Youth League.

He did not address the debt burden the project would put on the fiscus, the run it would put on foreign investment (given that the bulk of the mines are foreign-owned), or how state involvement in the mines would kill the competitive edge that exists in the private sector. Instead, he based his argument on a populist line and gave it an emotional and ideological appeal in favour of the masses. He was talking directly to the poor, wrapping them up in the sly notion that the only means to rid themselves of the shackles of poverty would be to share out the wealth by wrenching it from the hands of the whites. And so far, the masses are giving him their rounded support in return.

Malema took the same tack with the protracted issue of land reform, which has lagged shamefully under consecutive ANC-led governments and become another lobbying favourite for him in selling his EFF brand. For any country on the African continent, land reform is one of the most critical projects for a government to get right when its people were so wrongfully dispossessed, as black South Africans were.

In 1994, the ANC-led government set itself the target to return 30 per cent of the land to the people within a twenty-year period. Fifteen years later, the government was forced to flag the fact that, with only 6 per cent of the land restored by 2009, the target would not be met. Again, Malema seized the opportunity his own party had presented to him and promised full redistribution of the land 'in our lifetime', and without financial compensation.

As far back as 2010, he had begun to radicalise his approach to land reform by talking up the idea of forcibly taking back the land. In neighbouring Zimbabwe it is called a 'land grab', but in South Africa, as he put it then, 'it's called "expropriation with compensation determined by the state"'. And if the seller doesn't like the offering price, 'then we take the land and give you nothing,' he warned, no doubt to loud applause in townships and backwaters all over the country. Radical though Malema's politics are, there are hundreds of thousands of South Africans to whom he appeals and for whom his populist harangues have resonance.

Hence by the time he reinvented himself as the socialist leader of the EFF, transformation had advanced little and his political messages had become more relevant, and radical. Added to nationalisation and land grabs were pledges to double the minimum wage, the value of all social grants, pensions and any other state handout wrapped up in a black socialist fantasy with no room for whites.

Many continue to insist it is racism on his part. It is, but it isn't. It is race-based. There is a difference, one that lies in the fact that Malema is exploiting the problem that race and racism have never been fully addressed in South Africa. So he has decided to exploit the racial context instead, just as he exploits the unsolved problems that continue to weigh on the state.

It is farcical, or as Mbembe pointed out earlier, it is carnivalesque. One can't help but wonder what might have been if there had been a show of solid leadership on the part of the ANC, or if someone with a more genuine political outlook than Malema had chosen to address the country's state of affairs. He simply made the most of an enormous gap in the country's politics and chose to throw up hasty solutions to complex problems that the state is struggling to deal with.

'And that's the danger,' says Vally. 'There will come a time when people will stop depending on the state and try to access the wealth and the land themselves. And who will they turn to? Malema.'

And that's what makes Malema what he is: a man with an uncanny ability to read the socio-economic conditions around him; a man with a past that can empathise with real hardship; a man who has been at the receiving end of race-based politics; and a man with a growing political power base.

It is a mix of the past and the present, of the psychosocial and the structural in a particular blend at a given time, that has given rise to Julius Malema, first as a democrat and later as a socialist, both political identities forged to suit his needs at a given time.

Bear in mind again the words of Karl Marx in *The Eighteenth Brumaire of Louis Bonaparte* that reflect on the reinvention of the

political past. But as Marx also noted in that text: 'Hegel remarks somewhere that all great world-historic facts and personages appear, so to speak, twice. He forgot to add: the first time as tragedy, the second time as farce.'[12]

Chapter 16

So that's Malema: Now this is the future

The last time I spoke to Malema was in the dying weeks of 2013, by which time the EFF was already showing strong signs of becoming a considerable threat to the existing political contenders, and though that strength had yet to be tested at the polls, the young party was growing in popularity on a daily basis as men and women of all ages began to dally with the promise of economic freedom. Even Malema's critics had come to concede that he was running on a winning ticket, but it was only when I spoke with him that afternoon that I qualified my own attitude towards his new party, and the birth pangs of South Africa's pending political crisis.

A politician will always think of the next election (unlike the statesman, who thinks of the next generation), and though he had yet to contest the 2014 vote, Malema was already burbling gaily about the local government elections that were scheduled to take place two years hence. Over the past few years, South Africans have become more pragmatic when electing a party or individual to run their municipality than when deciding on a party to lead the country, which often tends to be a more emotionally driven

process. Conversely, for an independent candidate or a young party that is trying to make its mark, the local government elections are infinitely easier to contest, for obvious reasons.

Even though the EFF was confident it would make inroads in the general elections of 2014, realistically the party knew it would not win a province and therefore would not be able to implement any of the radical policies promised to its followers. Though the leaders had introduced themselves to the electorate as the government-in-waiting on not one but several occasions, Malema privately conceded this was not in reference to 2014 but to a time in the not-too-distant future. The EFF was playing the long game of politics, and winning multiple municipalities in the 2016 local government elections was one of its core targets, which would work for the party on a number of levels: it would obviously give it political power, but it would also give access to public funds for administrative purposes, which would allow the EFF to extend its brand at the taxpayers' expense rather than its own.

Consider the exposure the EFF has had since it was elected to public office in the 2014 elections. It has been quite remarkable really, especially when the bulk of the coverage has little to do with politics and all to do with the deceptive garb of populism, in this instance the working-man's clothes. But consider too how the mechanics of public life have impacted on the party's grim finances. For example, there are twenty-five EFF MPs now earning salaries in the region of R1 million a year and, in accordance with the Sankara Oath and other party pledges, a not insignificant portion of those earnings is intended for the party's coffers. As public representatives, they were also given the use of parliamentary and provincial legislature offices, telephones, faxes, and so forth, in Cape Town and elsewhere in the country,

and though such services are intended for the purposes of public office, they are of significant and practical benefit to the likes of the fledgling EFF, as they are to any other party. Once it begins winning control of municipalities, as it surely will, Malema is of the view that the party will then begin to mirror the growth of the DA's very successful and steady trajectory from a humble municipal presence in the early days of apartheid to control of the Western Cape fifteen years later.

There is the understandable concern that the stiff competition the EFF will face en route will force it to radicalise its policies even further in order to capture more minds, clearly with dire consequences. As mentioned elsewhere, it is on the back of a radical and militant approach that the Association of Mineworkers and Construction Union has usurped the National Union of Mineworkers in the mining belt in the past few years, but at a tremendous cost to the sector. Just imagine the rancid populism of the EFF getting any worse than it already is.

In this race to the bottom, the alternative inspires little hope: an ANC battling a withering reputation and its party leader's impeachable incompetence as it entrenches its concept of a 'managed democracy'.

A 'managed democracy' is one that is democratic on paper but in practice is characterised by enhanced levels of autocracy and despotism. Indonesia practised a 'managed' or 'guided democracy' in the late 1950s. Modern-day Russia is also a 'managed democracy', as is Cambodia. The democracy that was celebrated by the ANC when the country marked its twentieth anniversary of freedom is light years away from the people-centred government the party promised when it came to power

in 1994 and, when examined more closely, its style of democracy is every bit as grim as those in the countries just mentioned.

In a talk he gave a few years ago, Nikolay Petrov of the Carnegie Moscow Center described a 'managed democracy' as one with a strong presidency but with weak institutions; state control of the media; control over elections; visible short-term effectiveness; and long-term inefficiency. Under a managed democracy, the system is highly dysfunctional and has poor information flows. The people are led by an iron-fisted and heavy-handed state and have little choice but to fall into line behind the powers that be. The end result is an unstable stability.

While business may boom in the private sector, corruption across the board becomes rife. The judiciary is co-opted. The electoral system weakens. Protests are nipped in the bud from very early on. A political elite emerges, shouldered by a private elite that is hand-plucked from society. But both elites are underpinned by shaky foundations and cannot endure.

'Like a mule, a managed democracy is an unnatural hybrid incapable of reproducing itself,' Petrov argued.

South Africa doesn't entirely fit Petrov's description, though there is a lot in it that rings true. The country still holds free and fair elections, unlike many other countries on the continent (though the scandal surrounding Pansy Tlakula, the chairperson of the Independent Electoral Commission, does afford cause for concern). However, parts of the judiciary have already fallen prey to political pressures, with some appointees caving in with little or no shame in what has been a slow but consistent onslaught on the part of the ANC for quite a number of years. Freedom of expression is also under heavy threat, either through the punitive secrecy bill or the way in which some big media houses are now owned by a Zuma-friendly clique, namely the Gupta family and Iqbal Survé.

Zuma's style of rule also undergirds the unfolding 'managed democracy'. He has tended to surround himself with individuals who are compromised in some way and by giving them back their power, he buys their loyalty. Most such appointments tend to be within the police force, the intelligence or justice departments or other security structures or, of late, in government departments where tender values are high.

The septuagenarian, who was an ANC spy during the apartheid era, is not alone in this; at least half of his cabinet are behind him in his ascendancy and support his restructuring of the government into a force rooted firmly in Zuma's influence.

Left unchecked, the ANC will transform South Africa into the kind of police state that Russia has become under Vladimir Putin. In the Soviet era, Putin had been a long-standing member of the KGB and resigned only days before the collapse of the Soviet Union in 1991. Seven years later, Boris Yeltsin appointed him as head of the Federal Security Service, or FSB, the main successor of the KGB. When Putin succeeded Yeltsin two years later, he filled the organisation with old friends, loyalists and KGB agents, and expanded their powers and their authority and grew the FSB into an elite, untouchable structure that helped him fight off his opponents to maintain his two-term presidency. They also supported his subsequent reincarnations as prime minister and more recently president. One book title aptly refers to the FSB as *The New Nobility*.

Putin also staffed the Kremlin with loyalists and ensured he had the right men and women in all of the key positions across the state and its various structures and throughout the corporate world, creating an elite and powerful band of officials commonly referred to as the *siloviki*, which loosely translates to 'power guys'. The *siloviki* control government, the private sector, public entities

and civil society. In effect, they run Russia and their thinking is the same throughout. They are extreme nationalists and very anti-Western in their outlook. Despite the fact that they were drawn from the Soviet era, they do not believe in communism. They were, after all, the men who began to rise as communism began to fall, but what they have taken from that communist era is a fierce need to control Russia. They are powerful where it matters to have clout and with their power has come the belief that no law or person is bigger than them in terms of achieving their mission.

Their equivalent in South Africa are the ANC's so-called cadres, who are deployed to all the arms of government, semi-state bodies, law enforcement agencies, the judiciary and the corporate sector. The formidable system of 'cadre deployment' may function like an employment agency, but it is designed 'to give black people operational exposure', in the words of the party's Secretary-General Gwede Mantashe.

And yet despite the similarities between South Africa and Russia, Zuma's desire is to emulate not Russia per se, but instead China. Under President Zuma's watch, the ANC has forged close ties with the Asian giant, and in the past couple of years dozens of party members have been sent to China to attend the Communist Party's political school, and plans are now being rolled out in South Africa to build a similar kind of institute.

However, as the ANC looks east it is not towards a system of communism or socialism, but instead at state corporatism, the system of governance and style of rule that the Chinese adopted during the reform era and which helped define its transition from a totalitarian to an authoritarian state over the past few decades.

An institutional mechanism employed by a state to regulate society, rather than an ideology within a political system,

state corporatism has been associated with some of the most repressive regimes in the world and is widely regarded as the least palatable 'ism' of them all.

In the Chinese context, it helped the Asian communist nation make a fiercely controlled shift out of its dark ages towards a slightly more liberated state of affairs. In the South African context, however, and moving along the same spectrum, though from the opposite end, state corporatism is facilitating a gradual shutdown of the democratic space that was created in 1994.

South Africa is still a democracy in name and constitution. In practice, however, it is beginning to take on another form that can often be hard to fathom or frame, and state or authoritarian corporatism often helps to define some of the new grey areas.

Corporatism is a centuries-old concept that started out as a philosophy or agenda to organise society and its individuals into major groups or bodies, or corpora. Enormously broad in definition, almost to the point of defying it, corporatism therefore took on various forms down the centuries, across the political spectrum and in a multitude of contexts.

In its more extreme form, corporatism became the hallmark of regimes such as Benito Mussolini's in Italy. By the middle of the twentieth century, authoritarian corporatist states were emerging in Asia, in countries such as Japan, South Korea and Taiwan as they began to embark on intensive development and growth strategies.

By the latter half of the century, state and authoritarian corporatism had begun to give way to a more benign liberal or societal corporatism, which encouraged tripartite relations between government, the business sector and labour. It was a marked shift as societal corporatism began to lay the foundation for social pacts in various European and Scandinavian countries in the 1970s.

Towards the end of the apartheid regime, South Africa was ripe for liberal corporatism and it was from a tripartite union of voices and power groups from business, government and labour that the National Economic Development and Labour Council (NEDLAC) was eventually formed in 1994, building on the promise of a consensus democracy.

Little is left of that approach today, however. How much more control the ruling party intends to exert over South African life is not yet apparent; nor is it clear to what extent it could succeed, if at all, in copying the Chinese model of governance, as the two countries are markedly different. Unlike South Africa, the millennia-old Chinese state is strong, intact and, in its current stage, likely to sustain itself for some decades to come. It has developed into an important world and economic power that rests on a powerful and centralised structure, the product of careful planning by the Chinese Communist Party (CCP).

A core component of modern-day Chinese planning was aggressive acceleration of capitalist development at the behest, ironically, of the communists. The high economic growth registered in the 1990s was driven by the private sector and the CCP was forced to openly admit that it needed a capitalist class to grow its economy. But rather than compete with or curb the new economic elite, most of whom were products of the CCP anyway, in 2002 it formally invited them into its political structures, though they had been informally welcomed long before that. It was a strategic move that allowed the party to exert control over the business class and the economy, rather than have the capitalists control political reform, while the country continued to benefit from their economic interventions.

Today, China's moneymakers exist in parallel with the CCP, if not within it, and though they have fuelled the socio-economic

disparities that now define the country, they are an accepted and necessary class in the so-called communist nation.

That was the strength of the Communist Party: its capacity for reinvention without losing sight of itself in the process.

Despite its elite nature, the influence of the CCP across Chinese society is immense, due largely to the deployment of cadres in all walks of life who entrench the ideology and identity of the party as successfully as they helped roll out capitalism. A party representative sits on the board of every company and is also found within government departments and ministries, in addition to the appointed public servants. They oversee the judiciary, and are active in media houses, prominent in trade unions and generally present across all sectors. Though the ANC does likewise, China's deployed cadres are not only loyal party members but highly skilled and educated men and women fit for the task to hand. The same cannot be said of some of the key and often shameful appointments in South Africa.

Unlike the CCP, the ANC is not an elite structure and aggressively grows its membership at the kind of costs explained in earlier chapters. Nor does the ANC groom its future leaders in the way it used to or as the CCP does, but instead becomes embroiled in one succession battle after another, which steadily weakens it organisationally. Still, the ANC can count on a large degree of political autonomy for quite some time to come, something that the corporatist model requires.

What the ANC is lacking, though, is the backing of a state that is strong enough to enforce a corporatist system. The South African state has many fault lines, perhaps naturally so in Achille Mbembe's view. He defines it as a 'hybrid colossus' that encompasses the authoritarianism of the apartheid era, fragments of the new democratic culture and some of the cronyism of the bantustan.

When it is broken down into its constituent parts – the legislature, the judiciary and the executive – the judiciary is without doubt the strongest of the three arms, though its independence is being steadily eroded. The legislature, or parliament, is even less strong and is weakened by the country's political system of proportional representation, which hinders parliament's ability to hold the executive to account. With the ANC still resting on close to a two-thirds majority of the vote, its share of seats in parliament is allocated accordingly and therefore it effectively runs the legislature.

The executive is by far the weakest spoke and shows an inability and lack of capacity to deliver on what it promises and to perform in the manner it should, the core measure of any state. It is this very weakness that forced the term 'service delivery protests' into the South African lexicon in 2004.

Though a large number of key institutions – such as the electricity provider Eskom, television and radio outlets, a sizeable chunk of the rail and harbour system, and the Industrial Development Corporation, for example – remain under state control, the efficiency with which they are run is highly questionable, not helped by the high turnover of civil servants, which Hein Marais puts at 32 per cent nationally, which weakens the public service and state performance.

The state's grip over the economy is also weak, given its international make-up and the strong financial sector for which South Africa is renowned. The fact that so many of the large corporations are still controlled by whites does little to nurture solid state–capital relations.

There are pockets of efficiency, not least the South African Revenue Service (SARS), one of the biggest success stories since 1994 in the formal economy at least, and one of the best

tax collectors in the world. Though it is criticised by Marais 'as a highly centralised, top-down institute of compulsion' that operates in 'an authoritarian fashion and wields formidable punitive powers', perhaps not surprising given that it was 'rehabilitated with a (former) Leninist at the helm', he says, in reference to former SARS chief Pravin Gordhan,[13] it is hard to imagine a less authoritarian revenue collector being able to fulfil its mandate. The inability to collect taxes was, after all, one of the factors that led to the collapse of Greece.

The fact that more than 16 million people receive their social grants on time each week or month is further testament to public efficiency. That two of the country's three top metros – Cape Town and Durban – function successfully is another. People living in the rural areas can now access nearby offices to get their identity cards, for example – a marked improvement on former times when distance from urban life often meant the difference between being in the system and outside it.

However, when we consider the three main challenges facing the country today – job creation, education and security – the bigger picture appears dysfunctional. If the institutions designed to tackle these three challenges functioned at an acceptable level, and if sufficient vision, ambition and innovative thinking were in place, the country would not be beset with high crime, high unemployment and such poor education levels.

It is not beyond the South African state to address these deficiencies, but for as long as it continues to appoint politically connected rather than technically able people to key positions, it will continue to underperform and fail to reach its goals.

In China, when a party appointee underperforms he or she is not only removed from the position, but his or her political career is terminated, yet South Africa is laden with examples of

cadres ousted from various offices for some or other reason (often a criminally related one) only to be rewarded by reinstatement into their positions, or deployment to other equally high-ranking positions or a posting to one of the country's overseas embassies. When Zuma came to power and began to reconfigure the diplomatic corps on this basis, he was left with the most inefficient and unsuitable team of ambassadors on the African continent, something that members of the South African diplomatic corps and members of the African corps regard as a grave insult to continental relations.

What will happen when the ANC wakes up to the fact that it is not China and does not have the political or strategic strength to do as China does? Its followers will be the first to protest against unfulfilled promises and it is likely that authoritarian tendencies will begin to emerge as the frustrations of failure become apparent. Writing more than half a century ago, Frantz Fanon warned of the pitfalls of African nationalism post-liberation when the people become the enemy that feeds the rhetoric of nationalism.

Fifty years ago it led to dictatorships across the continent, but for the reasons explained above, that is unlikely in today's South Africa. Given the fault lines across the state, the corporatist model is likely to fail as well. What will most likely emerge, in an ANC-led country, instead is a 'managed democracy'. The vision is there. The '*siloviki*' are already in place. The elite have been identified. And that unnatural hybrid that Petrov talked of will surely come to pass.

So where will Malema fit into this hybrid? I would venture a prediction that he will never return to the ANC, regardless of what may come of the EFF. I would also venture a guess that the EFF will not become a national government, at least not in

Malema's lifetime. That, however, will not prevent him from causing significant damage nationwide. With charming pretence he has tapped into the frustrations and anger of the politically alienated and the socially and economically depressed, and it is not beyond him to lead the underclass in a permanent revolution against the authority of the ANC-led government. As he has said himself, 'This is a struggle between the future and the past', but in the present lies the sure prospect of immense tension and conflict, led by the militant army of the red berets.

In an exhibition he staged halfway through 2011, renowned pop artist Beezy Bailey looked at the iconic stature of Nelson Mandela.

In one installation he cast the old man in a large, open expanse. But instead of one Mandela there were several men walking through that landscape, each one cast in a different colour, as if personifying a rainbow.

Bailey called it a 'Rainbow Notion', then lent the name to the entire exhibition 'because the idea of the nation is struggling', he told me, 'so the idea of the notion seemed more fitting'.

When I asked him what imagery came to mind if he were to depict Julius Malema, then the rabble-rousing head of the Youth League, Bailey opted for 'a threshold'.

'I see him at a threshold,' he continued. 'On a cusp. He's in a beautiful garden. That garden is South Africa. It's full of beauty. But some of the fruits are poisonous. There's a slip in the path. And he can go down the dark side or the light side. He will use stuff from the dark side to get into power. But after that, we don't know. And that's precisely the point. We don't know. We're just watching. We're all on that threshold with him. And at the same time, he is that threshold.'

'So what about the rainbow notion?' I asked.

'Well, that's precisely it,' Bailey answered. 'Here is the old man cast in the rainbow across the country. The whole world is captured by the beauty and the utopia of it all. But it's not really working.

'And then I look at the young man, Malema. And I see the threshold. And he is the man who can make it a nation or just a notion.'

Acknowledgements

My thanks to a number of people, including Rehana Vally, Thabo Makunyane, Rayne Stroebel, Sisonke Msimang, Stefaans Brümmer and Craig McKune of the M&G investigative unit. To Achille Mbembe, Moeletsi Mbeki, Somadoda Fikeni and the late Heidi Holland. To IDASA and the Association of Non-Fiction Authors of South Africa. To the team at Picador Africa and, in particular, their publisher, Andrea Nattrass. And a special thank you to my sister, Edel.

My biggest thanks go to Julius Malema, who took me into his confidence and into his world in allowing me to relay his unauthorised biography. He did not like the first edition of this book. No doubt he will not like this edition either, but I hope he will at least agree that, overall, this is a fair portrayal of who he is.

Appendix

As I talk about in Chapter 8, on 20 July 2011 Julius Malema was sent a list of questions arising out of the research for this book. The most significant of these questions are shown below:

1. On 14 October 2009, when I shadowed you for a week and which provided the basis for two newspaper articles that subsequently appeared in the *Sunday Independent*, I asked you what was helping to foot your lifestyle. You said that you had no other income other than your ANC Youth League salary. Your words were 'No, this is it.' It would later emerge that you were also earning an income from SGL (see below).

1a. Why did you deny that extra income when I posed that question in October 2009?

1b. Have you ever declared your extra income to your employers, the ANC (ANC Youth League)?

2. What have been your sources of income over the past ten years (be it in the form of salary, gifts, donation, loans)?

3. Your colleague and friend Pule Mabe told me that together, you and him, 'did tenders', 'small tenders', many years ago. That information was offered voluntarily by Pule during an

interview I did with him in 2011, on your request, when I wanted to know about the early tenders you dabbled in. He told me that you and he won the following:

- A public tender to provide branded plastic bottles for Lepelle Water in Limpopo. Please confirm the amount you earned from this tender. Please confirm how this tender was won.
- A public tender to supply uniforms at your old high school, Mohlakaneng (which you had also confirmed to me). Please confirm the amount you earned from this tender. Please confirm how this tender was won.
- A public tender to supply uniforms at a school in Dendron. Please confirm the amount you earned from this tender. Please confirm how this tender was won.
- A public tender to organise the inauguration of a mayor in the Waterberg district of Limpopo (which you also confirmed to me). Please confirm the amount you earned from this tender. Please confirm how this tender was won.

4. How much did you earn from the public tenders you won through the South African Rail Commuter Corporation (SARCC)? Please confirm how this tender was won.

5. You have been officially linked to the following legal entities in a business capacity:

- SGL Engineering Projects
- SGL Engineering Projects CC
- Segwalo Consultancy Engineers
- Segwalo

- 101 Junjus
- Ever Roaring
- Blue Nightingale
- Ngape Mining Investments
- (You have separately told me you are involved in On-Point.)

Please detail the income you have earned from them since they were legally established, including the source of each income and, if they resulted from tenders, whether you brokered the tenders or took any action to influence the award of the tender in favour of the entity concerned.

6. You told me on two occasions you are involved in On-Point (something the media recently reported on). What is your shareholding in that company? If it is not a shareholding, in what way are you financially involved in On-Point?

7. You are also linked to another legal entity – the Ratanang Family Trust – of which you are both a donor and a trustee on behalf of your son Ratanang Ramohlale – and which you established on 25 October 2007 (the name of the trust hangs on a plaque outside the church you donated to the people of Seshego). Has the Ratanang Family Trust earned any income since 2007, by way of properties or other assets attached to it or monies lodged into its accounts?

8. I understand that in 2004 a meeting took place at the Sterpark home of Matome Sathekge of Bakgaloka Building Construction and among those present were yourself and the two directors of SGL. Please explain the outcome of that meeting and how it linked you to SGL.

8a.   Did you ever help or ensure that SGL won tenders from 2004 through to the present day (even though SGL now operates as On-Point)?

8b.   If so, did you receive any financial reward for doing that?

8c.   If so, how much did you receive in terms of a commission for each tender you may have helped SGL win?

8d.   If you were paid such a commission, how was that money paid out to you (e.g., cash, cheque, etc.)?

9.   In 2006 your company Blue Nightingale became a 3 per cent shareholder in a venture that won a lucrative waste management public tender. The media subsequently reported that you were paid out for the equivalent of what your shareholding might have earned over the duration of the tender. However, I understand that that payout, in 2006, which was in excess of the amount listed by the media reports, was not a payout of the value of your shareholding but instead a loan.

9a.   Can you confirm that this is true?

9b.   If so, can you confirm the exact amount of that loan?

9c.   Have you repaid that existing loan, in full? If so, when?

9d.   It has also been explained to me that you requested that loan so as to build your mother a house (see below). Please confirm whether or not this is true.

9e.   I also understand that you remained as a shareholder of the firm until the waste management tender expired last year. Can you confirm if this is true?

9f.   If you remained a shareholder throughout this period, what was the total income you earned from this public tender?

10.   My understanding is that Blue Nightingale was a shareholder in a business arrangement with Beta Projects

and Beta Projects Consortium. Can you confirm the amount of the shareholding?

10a.   If so, please explain the nature of the arrangement and the public tenders it involved.

10b.   If so, please also explain the amount of money such an arrangement earned for Blue Nightingale.

11.   What public tenders did Ever Roaring win that would have linked the company to Vuna Health Care?

12.   You once stated – around the end of 2009/early 2010 – that your net salary as ANC Youth League president was slightly in excess of R40 000 per month. Yet at that time you were paying R18 000 each month in rent on your Sandown property at Silvela Road – prior to you purchasing it. When you took on the lease of that house, the agreement was R18 000 per month, plus a deposit equivalent to two months' rent. You paid the entire amount – one year's rent plus two months' deposit – up front, in a couple of bulk payments. Was this made possible by the extra income earned in addition to your ANC Youth League salary?

13.   You have been reported as saying in the press that you live on donations and handouts (*Mail & Guardian* article), which may partly explain the perception of wealth that has been created around you.

13a.   Who are your main donors?

13b.   If you are not prepared to divulge the names of such individuals to me, can I ask why not, given your political profile in South Africa today?

13c.   Do your donors expect anything in return for the money and/or gifts they give you?

13d. If so, what do they expect in return?

14. Have any of the businessmen who have donated money and/or gifts to you or who have paid for certain aspects of your life – as mentioned above – ever been linked to SGL (or any of its sister companies) or On-Point in any way?

14a. If said businessmen are not associated with SGL (or any of its sister companies) or On-Point today, have they been associated with those entities at any time in the past?

15. Has Martin Kingston ever donated any gifts or money to you?

15a. Did Martin Kingston give you money towards the down payment of your residence at 25 Silvela Road in Sandown?

15b. If he did not give you money towards the down payment of the house, did he give you money around the time that you purchased 25 Silvela Road in Sandown?

16. Are you linked to any loan account in any company or business entity that is currently operating in South Africa?

16a. Is the Ratanang Family Trust linked to any company or business entity that is currently operating in South Africa?

Properties

You have purchased a number of properties in the past few years, among them the following:

- A site at Sterpark in August 2006 for R222 000
- A house at 23 Mopane Street in Flora Park in May 2007 for R1 million (with a bond that has since been cleared)
- A house at 25 Silvela Road, Sandown, in August 2009 for R3.6 million, which has since been razed to the ground and is undergoing a reconstruction

- A farm in Palmietfontein in June 2010 for R900 000
- A house in Faranani Estate, also in June 2010, for R1.36 million

1.   What was the source of extra income and/or money that was available to you to purchase such properties?

2.   When you purchased the site at Sterpark it was from Matane Edwin Mphahlele. He had purchased it directly from the municipality for a price of R222 300 in August 2006. When it was eventually transferred to his name, it was immediately then transferred to your name for the same amount of R222 300.

2a.   How do you explain the fact that Mphahlele sold the site to you for the same price as he bought it, even though it was on prime land and he could have made a substantial profit on it?

2b.   The transfer documents bear consecutive numbers – T44230/2007 (Mphahlele) and T44231/2007. Why was this so?

2c.   The property was sold for R680 000 six months later, through a property agent. How much did you actually receive for the site after the property agent's cut was deducted? My understanding is that it is significantly less than what appeared on the deeds records.

3.   You then bought Mopani Street and took a bond out on that house. You carried out extensive renovations on house and property, including the erection of high walls around the house; the installation of a swimming pool; the erection of a lapa; new windows. How much did these renovations cost and who paid for them? If it was you, please explain the

source of that income, as my understanding is that at that time your only official source was your Youth League salary as provincial secretary.

4.   Do you have any financial interests in Gwama Properties?

Income tax

1.   Have you accurately declared all of your income that is taxable and that which is non-taxable?

2.   Have all of the legal entities with which you have been associated (as listed in 5 and above) fully declared their income to SARS and paid all outstanding and liable dues?

3.   Some of the cars you have driven in the past, or which have been driven by your security men on your behalf, have not belonged to you, but to other people known to you. Have you declared the cars as so-called perks for tax purposes?

4.   Based on the media scrutiny around your alleged lavish lifestyle, would you consider subjecting yourself to an independent audit, carried out by an independent audit firm of your choice, which would carry out an audit on your instruction and work towards giving you a clean due diligence report?

5.   Would you grant me permission to confirm with SARS that your returns are in order and up to date?

Notes

1. Bakhtin, Mikhail Mikhailovich, *Rabelais and His World*, p.7.
2. Shivambu, Floyd, *The Coming Revolution*, p.33.
3. Ibid., p.56.
4. Marx, Karl, *The Eighteenth Brumaire of Louis Bonaparte*, p.xx.
5. There was a suggestion from staff at the four-star Faircity Mapungubwe Hotel in downtown Johannesburg, where the EFF held many of its meetings, that the hotel bill was footed from an Australian bank account, though I don't know what truth is in that.
6. Those holding third-level qualifications include Julius Malema, Fana Mokoena, Leigh-Ann Mathys, Andile Mngxitama, Khanyisile Litchfield-Tshabalala, Floyd Shivambu, Mbuyiseni Ndlozi, Magdalene Moonsamy, Younus Vawda, Godrich Gardee and Reneiloe Mashabela.
7. Shivambu, Floyd, *The Coming Revolution*, p.66.
8. Fanon, Frantz, *Black Skin, White Masks*, p.89.
9. Ibid., p.64.
10. Ibid., p.68.
11. Ramphele, Mamphela, *Laying Ghosts to Rest*, pp.7–9.
12. Marx, Karl, *The Eighteenth Brumaire of Louis Bonaparte*, p.122.
13. Marais, Hein, *South Africa Pushed to the Limit*, p.350.

Select bibliography

Baai, Sandi. *O.R. Tambo: Teacher, Lawyer and Freedom Fighter* (Skotaville, 2006).

Bakhtin, Mikhail Mikhailovich. *Rabelais and His World*. Trans. by Helene Iswolsky (Indiana University Press, 1984).

Bunting, Brian. *Moses Kotane, South African Revolutionary: A Political Biography* (Inkululeko, 1975).

Callinicos, Luli. *Oliver Tambo: Beyond the Engeli Mountains* (David Philip, 2004).

Dubow, Saul. *The African National Congress* (Jonathan Ball, 2000).

Fanon, Frantz. *Black Skin, White Masks*. Trans. by Charles Lam Markmann (Pluto Press, 1986).

Limb, Peter. *The ANC's Early Years: Nation, Class and Place in South Africa before 1940* (Unisa Press, 2010).

Lodge, Tom. *Black Politics in South Africa since 1945* (Ravan, 1983).

Mandela, Nelson. *Long Walk to Freedom* (Abacus, 2002).

———. Quoting Walter Sisulu in the *Leaders* DVD series (produced and edited by Afravision).

Marais, Hein. *South Africa Pushed to the Limit: The Political Economy of Change* (UCT Press, 2011).

Marx, Karl. *The Eighteenth Brumaire of Louis Bonaparte*. First published in the first issue of *Die Revolution*, 1852, New York. Online version: Marxists Internet Archive (www. marxists.org).

Meli, Francis [Wellington Madolwana]. *South Africa Belongs to Us: A History of the ANC* (Zimbabwe Publishing House, 1988).

Norval, Morgan. *Inside the ANC: The Evolution of a Terrorist Organization* (Selous Foundation, 1990).

Ramphele, Mamphela. *Laying Ghosts to Rest: Dilemmas of the Transformation in South Africa* (Tafelberg, 2008).

Shivambu, Floyd. *The Coming Revolution: Julius Malema and the Fight for Economic Freedom* (Jacana, 2014).

Unger, Jonathan and Anita Chan. 'China, Corporatism and the East Asian Model'. *Australian Journal of Chinese Affairs* 33 (1995).

Walshe, Peter. *The Rise of African Nationalism in South Africa* (Donker, 1987).

Wiardia, Howard. *Corporatism and Comparative Politics: The Other Great Ism* (M.E. Sharpe, 1996).

Willan, Brian. *Sol Plaatje: Selected Writings* (Wits University Press, 1997).

Interviews conducted by the author

Beezy Bailey; Terry Bell; Max du Preez; Stephen Friedman; John Githongo; Ronnie Kasrils; Jeff Legodi; Tom Lodge; Pule Mabe; Siviko Mabunda; Winnie Madikizela-Mandela; Lebogang Maile; the late Henry Makgothi; Thabo Makunyane; Julius Malema; Maropeng Malema; Sarah Malema; Tshepo Malema; Frank Maponya; Lawrence Mapoulo; Matlala Maremane; Lehlogonolo Masoga; David Masondo; Cassel Mathale; the late Joe Matthews; Fikile Mbalula; Achille Mbembe; Andrew Mlangeni; Moshoeshoe Monare; Kenny Morolong; Clifford Motsepe; Sydney Mufamadi; Thomas Namathe; Patti Nkobe; Aziz Pahad; Freddie Ramaphakela; Sam Rampedi; Daisy Sebate; Jackie Selebi; Gillian Slovo; Vuyiswa Tulelo; Rehana Vally. (A further twenty-seven people were interviewed for this book, but because of the fear and loathing referred to in its pages, they asked not to be named.)

For Moya and Mum

Still an Inconv